Lecture Notes in Artificial Intelligence (LNAI)

Vol. 345: R. T. Nossum (Ed.), Advanced Topics in Artificial Intelligence. VII, 233 pages. 1988.

Vol. 346: M. Reinfrank, J. de Kleer, M. L. Ginsberg, E.Sandewall (Eds.), Non-Monotonic Reasoning. Proceedings, 1988. XIV, 237 pages. 1989.

Vol. 347: K. Morik (Ed.), Knowledge Representation and Organization in Machine Learning. XV, 319 pages. 1989.

Vol. 353: S. Hölldobler, Foundations of Equational Logic Programming. X, 250 pages. 1989.

Vol. 383: K. Furukawa, H. Tanaka, T. Fujisaki (Eds.), Logic Programming '88. Proceedings, 1988. IX, 251 pages. 1989.

Vol. 390: J. P. Martins, E. M. Morgado (Eds.), EPIA 89. Proceedings, 1989. XII, 400 pages. 1989.

Vol. 395: M. Schmidt-Schauß, Computational Aspects of an Order-Sorted Logic with Term Declarations. VIII, 171 pages. 1989.

Vol. 397: K. P. Jantke (Ed.), Analogical and Inductive Inference. Proceedings, 1989. IX, 338 pages. 1989.

Vol. 406: C. J. Barter, M. J. Brooks (Eds.), AI '88. Proceedings, 1988. VIII, 463 pages. 1990.

Vol. 418: K. H. Bläsius, U. Hedtstück, C.-R. Rollinger (Eds.), Sorts and Types in Artificial Intelligence. Proceedings, 1989. VIII, 307 pages. 1990.

Vol. 419: K. Weichselberger, S. Pöhlmann, A Methodology for Uncertainty in Knowledge-Based Systems. VIII, 132 pages. 1990.

Vol. 422: B. Nebel, Reasoning and Revision in Hybrid Representation Systems. XII, 270 pages. 1990.

Vol. 437: D. Kumar (Ed.), Current Trends in SNePS – Semantic Network Processing System. Proceedings, 1989. VII, 162 pages. 1990.

Vol. 444: S. Ramani, R. Chandrasekar, K. S. R. Anjaneyulu (Eds.), Knowledge Based Computer Systems. Proceedings, 1989. X, 546 pages. 1990.

Vol. 446: L. Plümer, Termination Proofs for Logic Programs. VIII, 142 pages. 1990.

Other volumes of the Lecture Notes in Computer Science relevant to Artificial Intelligence:

Vol. 231: R. Hausser, NEWCAT: Parsing Natural Language Using Left-Associative Grammar. II, 540 pages. 1986.

Vol. 232: W. Bibel, Ph. Jorrand (Eds.), Fundamentals of Artificial Intelligence. VII, 313 pages. 1986. Reprint as Springer Study Edition 1987.

Vol. 238: L. Naish, Negation and Control in Prolog. IX, 119 pages. 1986.

Vol. 256: P. Lescanne (Ed.), Rewriting Techniques and Applications. Proceedings, 1987. VI, 285 pages. 1987.

Vol. 264: E. Wada (Ed.), Logic Programming '86. Proceedings, 1986. VI, 179 pages. 1987.

Vol. 265: K. P. Jantke (Ed.), Analogical and Inductive Inference. Proceedings, 1986. VI, 227 pages. 1987.

Vol. 271: D. Snyers, A. Thayse, From Logic Design to Logic Programming. IV, 125 pages. 1987.

Vol. 306: M. Boscarol, L. Carlucci Aiello, G. Levi (Eds.), Foundations of Logic and Functional Programming. Proceedings, 1986. V, 218 pages. 1988.

Vol. 308: S. Kaplan, J.-P. Jouannaud (Eds.), Conditional Term Rewriting Systems. Proceedings, 1987. VI, 278 pages. 1988.

Vol. 310: E. Lusk, R. Overbeek (Eds.), 9th International Conference on Automated Deduction. Proceedings, 1988. X, 775 pages. 1988.

Vol. 315: K. Furukawa, H. Tanaka, T. Fujisaki (Eds.), Logic Programming '87. Proceedings, 1987. VI, 327 pages. 1988.

Vol. 320: A. Blaser (Ed.), Natural Language at the Computer. Proceedings, 1988. III, 176 pages. 1988.

Vol. 336: B. R. Donald, Error Detection and Recovery in Robotics. XXIV, 314 pages. 1989.

Lecture Notes in Artificial Intelligence

Subseries of Lecture Notes in Computer Science
Edited by J. Siekmann

Lecture Notes in Computer Science

Edited by G. Goos and J. Hartmanis

Editorial

Artificial Intelligence has become a major discipline under the roof of Computer Science. This is also reflected by a growing number of titles devoted to this fast developing field to be published in our Lecture Notes in Computer Science. To make these volumes immediately visible we have decided to distinguish them by a special cover as Lecture Notes in Artificial Intelligence, constituting a subseries of the Lecture Notes in Computer Science. This subseries is edited by an Editorial Board of experts from all areas of AI, chaired by Jörg Siekmann, who are looking forward to consider further AI monographs and proceedings of high scientific quality for publication.

We hope that the constitution of this subseries will be well accepted by the audience of the Lecture Notes in Computer Science, and we feel confident that the subseries will be recognized as an outstanding opportunity for publication by authors and editors of the AI community.

Editors and publisher

Lecture Notes in
Artificial Intelligence

Edited by J. Siekmann

Subseries of Lecture Notes in Computer Science

446

Lutz Plümer

Termination Proofs
for Logic Programs

Springer-Verlag
Berlin Heidelberg New York London
Paris Tokyo Hong Kong Barcelona

Author
Lutz Plümer
Universität Dortmund, Fachbereich Informatik
Postfach 50 05 00, D-4600 Dortmund 50, FRG

CR Subject Classification (1987): D.2.4, F.3.1, F.4.1, I.2.2–3

ISBN 3-540-52837-7 Springer-Verlag Berlin Heidelberg New York
ISBN 0-387-52837-7 Springer-Verlag New York Berlin Heidelberg

CONTENTS

Preface

This volume presents a technique for the automatic generation of termination proofs for logic programs. Such proofs can easily be achieved as long as recursive calls operate on arguments which are proper subterms of those originally given. If a procedure operating on recursive data structures has local variables in its recursive literals, termination proofs are difficult. Simplification orderings, which are often used to prove termination of term rewriting systems, are not sufficient to handle these cases. We therefore introduce the notion of linear predicate inequalities. These compare the sizes of tuples of terms of literals occurring in the minimal Herbrand model of a program. Term sizes are measured by linear norms. A technique for the automatic derivation of valid linear inequalities is described. This technique is based on the concept of AND/OR dataflow graphs. An algorithm which uses linear inequalities in termination proofs is given. The assumption that all recursion is direct keeps our approach efficient. We show, however, how mutual recursion can be eliminated by static program transformation. Finally we discuss how the scope of our technique can be enlarged by the integration of unfolding techniques.

This book is a slightly revised version of my thesis [PLU89]. It is based on research carried out within the EUREKA project EU 56 PROTOS. Research has been made possible by a grant from the Minister für Wissenschaft und Forschung des Landes Nordrhein-Westfalen. Partners of the PROTOS project, which started in April 1987 for a duration of three years, have been ETH Zürich, Schweizerische Bankgesellschaft, Sandoz AG, Belgian Institute of Management, IBM Deutschland, Universität Dortmund and Universität Oldenburg.

I am indebted to A. B. Cremers who inspired and supervised this research. I thank H. Ganzinger for his interest in this work and for many fruitful comments. Thanks also go to the colleagues from the "Logic Programming Group", namely W. Burgard, E. Eder, S. Lüttringhaus and A. Ultsch, and to the co-researchers of the PROTOS project. Discussions with R. Barbuti and M. Martelli during a research visit at the University of Pisa helped to clarify some of the ideas presented here. M. Schmidt deserves special thanks for manifold assistance including the software implementation of the techniques described in this book. Thanks also to Birgit Hühne for her careful grammatical proofreading.

Dortmund, April 1990   Lutz Plümer

Chapter 1

INTRODUCTION

Prolog has been advocated as a language which allows to write executable specifications. Unfortunately, when a correct specification in the form of a logic program is evaluated by a Prolog interpreter, problems may arise. Due to its depth-first search strategy the Prolog interpreter may enter infinite branches and thus miss solutions. A general technique which detects such problems in advance would be highly desirable.

The undecidability of the halting problem for Turing machines dictates that there is no algorithm which identifies exactly all terminating programs. Since every Turing computable function can be computed by a (pure) Prolog program, loop checking is undecidable for Prolog. A reasonable intention, however, is to identify sufficient criteria for termination which are strong enough to cover cases of practical interest. Moreover, techniques are desired which eliminate unnecessary and undesired loops either by program transformation or by adequate powerful control strategies.

Due to the lack of control constructs such as *goto, while ... do* or *loop ... exit,* as can be found in procedural languages, logic programs have recursion as the only potential source of infinite computations. As a matter of fact, this and the absence of side effects make the problem of automatic termination proofs tractable, compared to the difficulties encountered with programs written in an imperative language.

Informally, a recursive specification of a problem solving process says how to reduce a problem to a smaller one of the same kind. A termination proof gives evidence of the fact that the recursive instance of a problem is indeed easier to solve than the original problem. The basic approach, which goes back to [FLO66], is to give a termination function which identifies a decrease in argument size for each recursive call according to some well founded set.

For logic programming it has to be verified that all derivations in a proof attempt are of finite length. This requires specification of the strategy which guides the search for derivations. In this book we consider Prolog's depth-first-left-first strategy with backtracking. More sophisticated strategies, as for instance OLDT, are discussed as well.

It turns out very soon that termination of a given procedure depends on the pattern of argument bindings by which this procedure is invoked. This observation is illustrated by the following introductory example:

1.1 EXAMPLE: *Append*

a_1:   append([], L, L).
a_2:   append([H|L$_1$],L$_2$,[H|L$_3$]) $\leftarrow$ append(L$_1$,L$_2$,L$_3$).

  Goal: $\leftarrow$ append(X,Y,Z)

The goal $\leftarrow$ append(X,Y,Z) represents different kinds of queries, depending on how X, Y and Z are bound.

If X and Y are ground lists, then Z will be bound to a ground list which is the concatenation of X and Y. During the computation of Z append is always called with its first two arguments ground. In this case clause a_2 says that the problem of concatenating [H|L$_1$] and L$_2$ can be reduced to the problem of concatenating L$_1$ and L$_2$ which is indeed a smaller problem. Thus the evaluation of this kind of query terminates.

The same is true if Z is bound to a list of ground elements. In this case the evaluation of the query $\leftarrow$ append(X,Y,Z) will split Z into X and Y. In this case, append is always called with its third argument bound to a ground term. If Z is not the empty list, this query will give a finite number of different answers. The evaluation of this query terminates since the problem of splitting [H|L$_3$] is reduced to the smaller problem of splitting L$_3$.

The situation is different if Y is bound to a list of ground elements, while X and Z are free variables. In this case the query $\leftarrow$ append(X,Y,Z), which asks for a list Z with suffix Y and corresponding prefix X, has an infinite number of different answers. This gives rise to a nonterminating computation.

The characterization of a procedure as terminating or nonterminating requires informations about the "modes" of argument bindings by which this procedure is invoked. The recognition of the termination of append in its 'concatenation' mode is straightforward since the term L_1 is a proper subterm of $[H|L_1]$ irrespective of variable bindings.

The case is not so easy for the next small program, specifying the permutation of lists:

1.2 EXAMPLE: *Permutation*

p_1:   perm([],[]).
p_2:   perm(L,[H|T]) ←   append(V,[H|U],L),
                          append(V,U,W),
                          perm(W,T).

We assume that perm is invoked with its first argument ground. The first clause says that the empty list is a permutation of itself. The second clause says how to handle a nonempty list L: split it into two sublists V and [H|U], and concatenate V and U to get W. Thus W is derived from L by removing an inner element. If now T is a permutation of W, [H|T] is a permutation of L.

The difficulty in achieving a termination proof for the perm-procedure is that it is not obvious that the list, to which W will be bound when perm(W,T) is invoked, is smaller than the list L originally given. It can be recognized, however, if one takes the semantics of append into account. This can be done by giving an inequality relating the sizes of the arguments of append. In our case it is sufficient to know that for every correct answer for a goal ← append(A,B,C) the sum of the lengths of the lists A and B cannot be less than the length of C, and vice versa.* In this case append(V,[H|U],L) shows us that the sum of the lengths of the lists V and U is strictly smaller than the length of L, and append(V,U,W) shows that the length of W is smaller than or equal to the sum of the lengths of V and U. Thus we have that the length of W is strictly smaller than the length of L.

In the perm-example the variable W represents an "input" of the recursive call of perm(W,T) which has been computed by the subgoal on its left. Such a variable will be

---

* In this example, of course, there is equality between the lengths of A plus B and the length of C. This is a special case, however.

called "local". The problem of local variables has to be approached in order to achieve non-trivial termination proofs for logic programs.

This book presents a technique for the generation of termination proofs for logic programs which is based on the automatic generation of linear inequalities for predicates. Linear inequalities allow to handle occurrences of local variables. While the overall approach of our algorithm is similar to the approach of a technique recently given by Ullman and van Gelder [ULG88], it is more general in several important respects.

This book is organized as follows:

Chapter 2 presents basic notions.

Chapter 3 starts with defining syntactic program properties, aiming mainly at characterizing different aspects of recursion. It introduces several concepts which can be used to describe the static semantics of a logic program: modes, types and predicate inequalities. Unfolding as an important technique for program transformation is discussed as well.

Chapter 4 approaches the problem of termination of logic programs on a more general level. It starts with a theoretical characterization of terminating logic programs, using Clark's notion of proof trees and concepts introduced by Vasak and Potter. Structural and primitive recursion indicate cases where termination can be verified by more or less syntactical analysis. On the other hand, the concept of bounded recursion discussed in 4.5 includes the possibility of undesired loops which can be avoided by strategies more sophisticated than SLD-resolution. OLDT-resolution is discussed as an example of such a strategy.

Chapter 5 deals with the problem of local variables. From a principal point of view they are not really necessary. We give a theorem stating that everything which can be done with local variables can also be done without. On the other hand we will argue that elimination of local variables by program transformation does not facilitate the task of proving program termination.

Provided that linear predicate inequalities are given, chapter 6 shows how to use them. The notion of AND/OR dataflow graphs is introduced as the main data structure which allows to derive size relations between variables occurring in compound goals from given predicate inequalities.

Chapter 7 describes the automatic derivation of linear predicate inequalities and gives an algorithm proving termination of logic programs using such inequalities. There is also a discussion on efficiency and implementation aspects.

Chapter 8 discusses several terminating procedures where the algorithm given in chapter 7 is unable to prove termination and shows how to improve this algorithm by program transformation. The preceding chapters assume that the programs to be analyzed have only direct recursion. Here we discuss two techniques which eliminate mutual recursion. This chapter also contains a comparison with techniques known so far.

Chapter 9 summarizes what is substantial from our point of view, and poses problems for further research.

Chapter 2

BASIC NOTIONS

This chapter presents the basic notation used throughout the book. If not explicitly given here, definitions of logic programming terms can be found in [Llo87].

2.1 Logic Programs

We start by giving the definition of well-formed formulas for first order predicate logic. We first give an inductive definition of *terms*:

- A variable is a term.
- A constant, i.e., a function symbol with arity 0, is a term.
- If f is a n-ary function symbol and $t_1...t_n$ are terms, then $f(t_1,...,t_n)$ is a term.

An *atomic formula*, or an *atom* for short, has the form $p(t_1,...,t_n)$, where p is an n-ary predicate and $t_1...t_n$ are terms.

A *(well-formed) formula* is inductively defined as follows:

(a) An atomic formula is a well-formed formula.

(b) If F and G are formulas, then so are $\neg F$, $F \wedge G$, $F \vee G$, $F \rightarrow G$, and $F \leftrightarrow G$.

(c) If F is a formula and x is a variable, then $(\forall x\ F)$ and $(\exists x\ F)$ are formulas.

The symbols $\neg$, $\wedge$, $\vee$, $\rightarrow$ and $\leftrightarrow$ are called connectors, $\forall$ and $\exists$ are called quantifiers. Their informal semantics is as follows: $\neg$ is negation (not), $\wedge$ is conjunction (and), $\vee$ is disjunction (or), $\rightarrow$ is implication (if...then) and $\leftrightarrow$ is equivalence (iff, if and only if). $\exists x$ means "there is an x ..." and $\forall x$ means "for all x...".

The scope of $\forall x$ (resp. $\exists x$ F) in $\forall x$ F (resp. $\exists x$ F) is F. A *bound* occurrence of a variable in a formula is an occurrence immediately following a quantifier or an occurrence within the scope of a quantifier, which has the same variable as that one immediately after the quantifier. Any other occurrence of a variable is *free*.

For a formula F $\forall$ (F) denotes the *universal closure* of F, which is the closed formula obtained by adding a universal quantifier for every variable having a free occurrence in F. Similarly $\exists$(F) denotes the *existential closure* of F, which is obtained by adding an existential quanitfier for every variable having a free occurrence in F.

A *literal* is an atom or a negated atom.

A *program clause* has the form

$$A \leftarrow L_1,...,L_n$$

where A is an atom and $L_1,...,L_n$ are literals. A is called the *head*, $L_1,...,L_n$ is called the *body* of the clause. A clause with an empty body is called a *unit clause*. If all the $L_1,...,L_n$ are atoms, the clause is called *definite* or *Horn clause*.

A logic *program* P is a set of program clauses. If all program clauses are definite, the program is called *definite*.

In this book we will mainly be concerned with definite programs. If nothing else is explicitly stated, clauses and programs are implicitly assumed to be definite.

There is an obvious association of a logical formula to a logic program P. One simply considers P to be a conjunction of the formulas

$$\forall \tilde{x}: \quad A \ \vee \ \neg L_1 \vee \ \neg L_2 \ ... \ \vee \ \neg L_n$$

corresponding to the clauses

$$A \leftarrow L_1,...,L_n$$

in P where $\tilde{x}$ denotes the list of all variables in the clause. We denote this formula by $\hat{P}$.

In accordance with the standard notation of Prolog, variables will be denoted with the first character in upper case, while function and predicate symbols will be denoted with the first character in lower case.

An expression is either a term, a literal or a conjunction or a disjunction of literals.

We use a tilde $\tilde{}$ to denote a tuple or sequence of expressions. For example $\tilde{x}$ may denote a tuple of variables, $\tilde{t}$ will denote a tuple of arbitrary terms and $\tilde{L}$ may denote a sequence of literals.

Expressions which contain no variables are said to be *ground*.

A *substitution* θ is a function mapping variables to terms which is the identity almost everywhere. This notion is extended to map syntactic objects (such as terms, atoms or clauses) to syntactic objects by replacing all occurrences of variables x in the syntactic object by $x\theta$. A substitution is depicted by a set of pairs, such as $\{x_1/t_1,...x_n/t_n\}$. If θ has the form $\{x_1/y_1,...x_m/y_m\}$, where all the y_i are new and distinct variables, it is called a *renaming substitution*. If $t\theta$ is ground for an expression t, then θ is called a ground substitution or *instantiation* for t. For a (ground) substitution θ $t\theta$ is called *(ground) instance* of t.

A substitution α is said to be more general than a substitution β if $\beta = \alpha \circ \gamma$ for some substitution γ.

A substitution θ is a *unifier* of expressions A and B if $A\theta \equiv B\theta$. A = B says that there exists a unifier for A and B. In this case we say that A and B are unifiable.

If A and B are unifiable, then there exists a *most general unifier* mgu(A,B), which is unique up to variable renaming.

A *variant* of an expression is obtained by applying a renaming substitution to the expression.

A goal is a logical expression of the form $\leftarrow G_1,...,G_n$, where $G_1...G_n$ are literals. If the $G_1...G_n$ are all atoms, then the goal is called *definite*, which, again, will implicitly be assumed in the following.

The closure of a program P, written closure(P), is the set of all instances of clauses of P.

The set of ground terms which can be constructed from the function symbols occurring in a program P is called the *Herbrand universe HUP* of P. The set of ground atomic formulas which can be constructed from the predicate and function symbols occurring in P is called the *Herbrand base HBp* of P.

A *Datalog* program is a logic program which contains no function symbols of arity greater than 0.

A literal which has p as its predicate symbol is referred to as *p-literal*. A clause with a p-literal as its head is said to be a p-clause.

The subset of all p-clauses of a program is called the *procedure definition* π_p for p. From a logical point of view, π_p is a set of clauses. With regard to Prolog, however, a total ordering among the clauses of π_p is assumed.

For an expression E var(E) denotes the set of variable occurrences in E and vars(E) denotes the m u l t i set of variable occurrences in E.

A term or a literal is called normalized if no $v \in$ var(E) occurs more than once in vars(E). A clause is normalized if all its literals are normalized. A program is normalized if all its clauses are normalized.

The language of a program P is the set of all function symbols and predicate symbols occurring in P.

2.2 Model theoretic and fixed point semantics

There are several ways to give a meaning to a logic program. One way is to regard the set of all logical consequences of $\hat{P}$.

An *interpretation* of a closed well-formed formula F consists of a nonempty domain D and an assignment of "values" to each constant, function symbol, and predicate symbol occurring in F as follows:

- To each constant (i.e., 0-ary function symbol) an element of D is assigned.
- To each n-ary function symbol a mapping from the cartesian product D^n to D is assigned.
- To each n-ary predicate symbol a mapping from D^n to {true, false} (or equivalently, a relation on D^n) is assigned.

For an interpretation I with a domain D a closed well-formed formula gets a truth value, true or false, according to the following rules:

- The truth value of a closed atomic formula is given by the interpretation I.
- If the formula has the form ¬F, F∨G, F∧G, F→G or F↔G, then its truth value is evaluated according to table 2.2.1.
- If the formula has the form ∃x F then its truth value is true if there exists an d∈ D such that Fσ is a closed formula with truth value true, where σ={x/d}.
- If the formula has the form ∀x F, then its truth value is true if for all d∈ D Fσ is a closed formula with truth value true, where σ={x/d}.

Note that only closed formulas can be evaluated to true or false.

A closed formula G is *consistent* or *satisfiable* if there exists an interpretation I which evaluates G to true. We also say that I satisfies G or that I is a *model* of G. We say that G is *valid* if every interpretation of G satisfies G. A formula G is a *logical consequence* of formulas F_1, F_2,...,F_n if every interpretation I, which satisfies $F_1 \wedge F_2 \wedge ... \wedge F_n$, satisfies G as well. The latter is the case if $F_1 \wedge F_2 \wedge ... \wedge F_n \wedge \neg G$ is inconsistent.

A *Herbrand interpretation HI_P* of a logic program P is an interpretation which satisfies the following:

- The domain of the interpretation is the Herbrand universe HU_P
- constants in HU_P are assigned to themselves.
- If f is an n-ary function symbol occurring in P, then the mapping from $(HU_P)^n$ to HU_P defined by $(t_1,...,t_n) \rightarrow f(t_1,...,t_n)$ is assigned to f.

F	G	¬F	F∧G	F∨G	F→G	F↔G
true	true	false	true	true	true	true
true	false	false	false	true	false	false
false	true	true	false	true	true	false
false	false	true	false	false	true	true

2.2.1 *Truth Table*

A Herbrand interpretation is a *Herbrand model* if it satisfies $\hat{P}$. It is a simple version of the Löwenheim-Skolem theorem that a logical formula in clausal form has a model if it has a Herbrand model. With regard to the semantic of logic programs, attention can therefore be restricted to Herbrand models. For the case of definite clauses, it has been pointed out by van Emden and Kowalski [EMK76] that the intersection of all Herbrand models is again a Herbrand model, which is the least one. We will denote it by M_P. Consequently the notion of ground atomic logical consequence can be captured by a single model, the *least Herbrand model M_P*. This approach to assigning meaning to logic programs is called *declarative* or *model theoretic semantics*.

The least Herbrand model M_P equals the least fixed point of a function T_P introduced in [EMK76]. T_P maps subsets of the Herbrand base to subsets of the Herbrand base and is defined as follows:

$$T_P(I) = \{A \in HB_P \mid \text{ there is a ground instance } A \leftarrow L_1,...,L_n \text{ of a clause in P such that } \{L_1,...,L_n\} \subseteq I \} .$$

Application of T_P corresponds to one-step forward chaining, using P, deriving ground atoms from ground atoms. T_P is continuous on the complete lattice of subsets of the Herbrand base ordered by set inclusion. Let $T_P \uparrow \omega$ denote the limit of the chain obtained by iteratively applying T_P to the empty set. It follows that $T_P \uparrow \omega = lfp(T_P)$, the least fixed point of T_P.

A main interest in logic programming is to have queries answered correctly. We next define the declarative concept of a correct answer.

A *queried program* $\Pi = (P,G)$ is a program P together with an initial goal G. It is definite if both P and G are definite, which will implicitly be assumed in the following. An answer substitution for Π is a substitution for variables of G.

Let the goal G of Π be $A_1,...,A_k$. A substitution θ is a *correct answer substitution* for G if $\forall ((A_1 \wedge ... \wedge A_k)\theta)$ is a logical consequence of P. A ground answer substitution is a correct answer substitution which makes $A_1 \wedge ... \wedge A_k$ ground.

2.3 SLD-Resolution

Let G be the goal $\leftarrow A_1,...,A_m,...,A_k$ and C be the clause $A \leftarrow B_1,...,B_q$. G' is derived from G and C using mgu θ if the following holds:

(a) A_m is an atom, called the *selected atom*, in G.

(b) θ is a most general unifier of A_m and A.

(c) G' is the goal $\leftarrow (A_1,...,A_{m-1},B_1,...,B_q,A_{m+1},...,A_k)\theta$

An *SLD-derivation* for Π consists of a (finite or infinite) sequence $G_0 = G, G_1,...$ of goals, a sequence $C_1, C_2...$ of variants of program clauses and a sequence $\theta_1, \theta_2,...$ of mgus such that each G_{i+1} is derived from G_i and C_{i+1} using θ_{i+1}.

A single derivation step is called *SLD-resolution*.

A *computation rule* uniquely determines which atom is selected for every goal in a derivation .

An SLD-derivation is infinite unless, for some goal G_i in the derivation, there is no next goal. There are two cases. The SLD-derivation is successful if G_i is empty. In this case it is called an *SLD-refutation* for the initial goal G. The second case occurs when the derivation is finitely failed. A derivation fails finitely if for some G_i no (variant of the) head of a clause unifies with the selected atom of G_i.

An SLD-derivation is *fair* if every atom that appears in the derivation is chosen at some step.

SLD-resolution is a refinement of the resolution inference rule given by Robinson [ROB65]. An inference rule is called *correct* or *sound* if only valid formulas are inferred. It is called *complete* if all valid formulas can be inferred. Resolution is sound and complete for logical formulas in clausal form. Soundness of SLD-resolution is directly implied by soundness of resolution. While SLD-resolution is incomplete for clauses in general, it is complete for Horn-clauses. SLD-refutations are linear proofs, while proofs are trees for resolution in general. So SLD-resolution is much more efficient. This efficiency, however, has its price. The price is that negative information cannot be expressed in Horn-clauses (see 2.4).

The *success set* of a definite program P is the set of all $A \in HB_P$ such that the queried program (P, A) has an SLD-refutation.

The success set is the procedural counterpart to the least Herbrand model. Soundness and completeness of SLD-resolution implies that the success set and the least Herbrand model of a program P are in fact equal. Similarily, there is a procedural counterpart of a correct answer.

A *computed answer* θ for a queried program $\Pi = (P,G)$ is the substitution obtained by restricting the composition of $\theta_1 \theta_2 ... \theta_n$ to the variables of G, where $\theta_1, \theta_2, ... \theta_n$ is the sequence of mgu's used in an SLD-refutation of Π. A soundness result for SLD-resolution says that every computed answer substitution is correct. A further completeness result is that for every correct answer substitution θ for Π there exists a computed answer σ for Π and a substitution γ such that $\theta = \sigma\gamma$.

Finding a refutation for a logic program needs a certain amount of searching. The search space for a logic program is a special type of tree, called SLD-tree.

An *SLD-tree* for a queried program $\Pi = (P,G)$ is a tree satisfying the following:

(a) Each node of the tree is a (possibly empty) definite goal.
(b) The root node is G.
(c) Let $A_1,...,A_m,...,A_k$ be a node in the tree and suppose that A_m is the selected atom. Then for each program clause $A \leftarrow B_1,...,B_q$ such that A_m and A are unifiable with mgu θ, the node has a child $\leftarrow (A_1,...,A_{m-1},B_1,...,B_q,A_{m+1},...,A_k)\theta$.
(d) Nodes which are the empty clause have no children.

Each branch of the SLD-tree is a derivation. Branches corresponding to successful derivations are called *success branches*, branches corresponding to infinite derivations are called *infinite branches*, and branches corresponding to failed derivations are called *failure branches*.

A leaf node of an SLD-tree is either the empty goal or a goal that immediately fails since the selected atom is not unifiable with any program clause. A *partial SLD-tree* for Π is a nonempty tree derived from an SLD-tree for Π by pruning certain subtrees. For a partial SLD-tree, nonempty leaf nodes do not necessarily fail immediately.

As is established in [LLO87] the existence of a refutation for a queried program does not depend on the computation rule. Thus a computation rule can be fixed in advance and

used to construct the SLD-tree. The computation rule has a great influence on the size
and structure of the SLD-tree. The following example, taken from [LLO87], shows that
finiteness of the SLD-tree depends on the computation rule.

2.3.1 EXAMPLE: *Transitivity*

1:    p(X,Z) ← q(X,Y), p(Y,Z).
2:    p(X,X).
3:    q(a,b).

Goal: ← p(X,b).

The left SLD-tree in figure 2.3.2 comes from the standard Prolog computation rule
(select the leftmost atom), the right one comes from a computation rule which always
selects the rightmost atom. The left tree is finite, whereas the right one is infinite. Both
of them, however, have two success branches corresponding to the answers {X/a} and
{X/b}.

A general result is that, for a given queried program, either every SLD-tree has
infinitely many success branches or every SLD-tree has the same number of finite
branches.

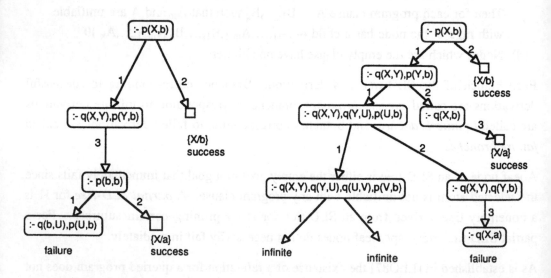

2.3.2 FIGURE: *SLD-trees for the program in 2.3.1*

A *search rule* is a strategy for searching SLD-trees to find success branches. Standard Prolog employs the computation rule which always selects the first literal of a goal together with a depth first search rule. Clauses are tried in the textual order they are given in the program. A search rule is called fair if it guarantees that each success branch on the SLD-tree will eventually be found. Note that Prolog's search rule is not fair.

2.4 SLDNF-Resolution

It is not possible to express negative information with Horn clauses. They state what is true but not what is false. SLD-resolution applied to Horn clauses can not deduce negative information. Let, for instance, $\Pi = (P,G)$ be a queried program where G consists of the single atom $A \in HB_P$. The formula $\neg A$ can not be a logical consequence of P since $P \cup \{A\}$ is satisfiable, having HB_P as model.

What can be done, however, is to introduce a new inference rule. One can state that if a ground atom A is not a logical consequence of a program, then $\neg A$ can be inferred. This inference rule is called the *Closed World Assumption (CWA)*. The Closed World Assumption is *categorical* for definite programs. This means that each ground atomic formula A in the language of the program (i.e., each $A \in HB_P$) is either true or false.

First order logic, however, is only semi-decidable. While it is possible to recursively enumerate all ground atoms A that are implied by a given program P, there is no algorithm which, for given A and P, decides in a finite number of steps whether or not A is a logical consequence of P. If A is not a logical consequence, a proof attempt may loop forever. Therefore in practice a weaker rule has to be applied. The *Negation as failure rule (NF)* says that $\neg A$ can be inferred if A is in the finite failure set of P. The *(SLD) finite failure set* of P is the set of all $A \in HB_P$ for which there exists a finitely failed SLD-tree for $(P,\leftarrow A)$.

It suffices to consider *any* fair SLD-tree to detect finite failure. An SLD-derivation is *fair* if it is either failed or if for every atom B in the derivation (some further instantiated version of) B is selected within a finite number of steps. An SLD-tree is fair if every branch of the tree is a fair SLD-derivation. It is shown in [LLO87] that if any fair SLD-tree fails for some queried program Π, then all fail.

To provide a semantical foundation for negation as failure, the *completion* P* of a logic program P has been introduced. The completion of a program is a conjunction of predicate definitions, each of the form

$$\forall \bar{x} \ p(\bar{x}) \ \leftrightarrow \ \exists \ \bar{y}_1 \ (\bar{x} = \tau_1 \wedge B_1)$$
$$\vee \exists \ \bar{y}_2 \ (\bar{x} = \tau_2 \wedge B_2)$$
$$...$$
$$\vee \exists \ \bar{y}_n \ (\bar{x} = \tau_n \wedge B_n)$$

corresponding to the procedure definition for p in P:

$$p(\tau_1) \ \leftarrow \ B_1.$$
$$p(\tau_2) \ \leftarrow \ B_2.$$
$$...$$
$$p(\tau_n) \ \leftarrow \ B_n.$$

where $\bar{y}_i$ denotes the variables in the ith clause above and each B_i is a (possibly empty) conjunction of atoms. If p does not appear in the head of a clause, then P* contains $\forall \bar{x} \ \neg p(\bar{x})$.

It is important to note that while $\hat{P}$ can never be inconsistent, P* may be.

An important result is that the ground facts which can be inferred to be false with the negation as failure rule are just those $A \in HB_P$ for which $\neg A$ is a logical consequence of P*. A proof can be found in [LLO87].

A fixed point characterization of the finite failure set FF_P can be given by

$$FF_P = \{A \in HB_P | \neg A \text{ can be inferred under the NF rule}\}$$
$$= HB_P - T_P \downarrow \omega,$$

where $T_P \downarrow \omega$ is the limit of the chain obtained by iteratively applying T_P to HB_P.

The CWA rule is more powerful than the NF rule. Unlike the CWA, the NF rule is not categorical: there are ground atoms where every SLD-tree contains no success path and at least one infinite path. If a definite program has a unique fixed point $T_P \uparrow \omega$ which is equal to $T_P \downarrow \omega$, then the CWA is equal to the NF rule. [BLA86] calls these programs *determined,* [BAM86] call these programs *ground-categorical.* The authors of these papers have adressed the search for conditions which are sufficient for this property as an open research problem. Such a sufficient condition will be given in chapter 7 *(restrained programs).*

Chapter 3

STATIC PROGRAM PROPERTIES AND TRANSFORMATIONS

In this chapter we discuss program properties which can be derived or verified by static analysis, namely

- modes,
- types, and
- linear predicate inequalities.

The automatic derivation of linear predicate inequalities is one of the main topics of this book. In this chapter, however, only basic definitions will be given.

We start this chapter by giving the notion of a predicate dependency graph which will help us to identify several forms of recursion.

3.1 Recursion

For two predicates p and q defined in a program P, we say p *depends* on q, written $p \rightarrow_{\pi} q$, if q occurs in the body of some of the clauses defining p. The relation '$\rightarrow_{\pi}$' defines the *predicate dependency graph* D_P of of the program P. Let '$\rightarrow_{\pi}^+$' denote the transitive and '$\rightarrow_{\pi}^*$' the reflexive and transitive closure of '$\rightarrow_{\pi}$'. We say that a p-literal L reaches q if $p \rightarrow_{\pi}^* q$, and a goal reaches q if it contains a literal which reaches q. A predicate p is a *recursive predicate* if $p \rightarrow_{\pi}^+ p$ holds. Two predicates p and q with $p \neq q$ are said to be *mutually recursive* if $p \rightarrow_{\pi}^+ q$ and $q \rightarrow_{\pi}^+ p$. We then write $q \leftrightarrow_{\pi}^+ p$.

Recursion which is not mutual is said to be direct. We further have $q \overset{*}{\underset{\pi}{\leftrightarrow}} p$ if $q \overset{+}{\underset{\pi}{\leftrightarrow}} p$ or $p = q$. Note that '$\overset{*}{\underset{\pi}{\leftrightarrow}}$' is an equivalence relation, partitioning the set of predicate symbols occurring in a program P into disjoint equivalence classes. This partition is given by the maximal strongly connected components of the predicate dependency graph D_p. A program is free of mutual recursion, or directly recursive, if every maximal strongly connected component has exactly one node.

Recall that in a directed graph $G(V,E)$ a strongly connected component (SCC) is a subgraph $G_i(V_i,E_i)$ such that two vertices v and w are in V_i if and only if in G there is a path from v to w and vice versa. Aho, Hopcroft and Ullman give an algorithm to find the maximal strongly connected components of a directed graph which is linear in the maximum of the numbers of edges and vertices of this graph [AHU74].

Figure 3.1.2 shows the predicate dependency graph of the program in example 3.1.1. Maximal strongly connected components are given by the node sets {b, c, d} and {e, f, g} corresponding to the fact that these predicates are mutually recursive.

If a program P has no mutual recursion, its predicate dependency graph induces a partial ordering $>_\pi$ which is definded as follows: $p >_\pi q$ if and only if $p \overset{+}{\underset{\pi}{\rightarrow}} q$ and $p \neq q$.

Let k be a clause in the definition π_p of a predicate p. A literal L in the body of k is called recursive if L reaches p. Let $\rho(k)$ denote the multiset of all recursive literals in the body of k. If $\rho(k)$ is not empty k is a recursive clause. The clause k is directly recursive if all elements of $\rho(k)$ have the same predicate as the head of k. If $\rho(k)$ is a singleton and k is directly recursive, k is called linear recursive. If all recursive clauses in π_p are linear recursive, p is called linear recursive. If $\rho(k)$ is empty, k is called exit clause. Obviously, all unit clauses are exit clauses.

a ← b.

b ← c.

c ← d.

d ← b.

a ← e.

e ← f.

f ← g.

g ← e.

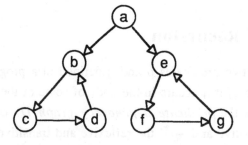

3.1.1 EXAMPLE
Mutual Recursion

3.1.2 FIGURE
Predicate Dependency Graph

3.2 Modes

In general, logic programs are undirected, i.e., there is no concept of *input* and *output* arguments to a procedure. An argument may be used either as an input or as an output argument, and procedures may be executed either in a "forward" or in a "backward" direction. Arguments of procedure calls may be partially instantiated, and computed answer substitutions may have variables, which are interpreted as being universally quantified (see 2.3).

Several authors have identified the fact that logic programs make no commitment as to the input or output of a procedure as the principal difference between the paradigms of logic and functional programming, see for instance [RED86] and [BLE86] .

It is often the case, however, that in a particular logic program a predicate is called in one direction only, i.e., it is called with a particular set of ground arguments (the input arguments), while another set of arguments may or may not be ground when the procedure is called, but will definitely be ground after the procedure has succeeded (the output arguments). Such information can, for instance, be used by a compiler. In the context of *compiling* and *optimization*, the interesting question is often whether a variable is ground, free or anything else at runtime [DEW88]. In our context of program *analysis*, we are merely interested in the question which arguments are guaranteed to be ground *before* a procedure is *called*, and which arguments are guaranteed to be ground *after a successful call* of a procedure. The following notions are similar to the ones given by Dembinski and Maluszynski in [DEM85].

A *mode* d_p for an n-ary predicate symbol p is a function from the set of indices $\{1,...,n\}$ to the set $\{+,-\}$. An $i \in \{1,...,n\}$ such that $d_p(i) = $ '+' $(d_p(i) = $ '-') is called *input (output) position* of p. A program (clause) with modes for all its predicates is called *moded*. The terms in(L) and out(L) denote the sets of variables occurring on the input and output positions of a literal L.

A *literal dependency graph* G_c for a moded clause $c = A :- B_1,...,B_n$ is a directed graph over the literals of c with arcs marked by sets of variables occurring in c. There is an arc $<L,M>$ in G_c marked by V if L and M are different literals of c and

- if $M \neq A$ and $V \neq \emptyset$, for $V = ($ out(L) $\cap$ in(M) $) \setminus$ in(A)
- if $M = A$ and $V \neq \emptyset$, for $V = ($ out(L) $\cap$ out(A) $) \setminus$ in(A)

G_c describes the *'flow of data'* among the body literals of c in a given mode. If L and M are body literals of c and there is an edge <L,M> labelled with V and v∈ V, then a binding for v is computed by L and passed as input to M. We say that M *depends* on L, and that v is *generated* by L and *consumed* by M. Variables occurring on input positions of the head of c are excluded since they will be assumed to be bound to ground terms when c is called.

A static dependency graph G_c for a moded clause $c = A \leftarrow B_1,\ldots,B_n$ is *full* if for every variable $v \in var(c) \setminus in(A)$ the following holds: There exists some $j \in \{1,\ldots,n\}$ and an arc $<B_j,B_i>$ marked with V containing v if $v \in in(B_i) \cup out(A)$ for some $i \in \{1,\ldots,n\}$.

That G_c is full essentially means that no variable occurs at an input position of a body literal or at an output position of the head literal unless it appears somwhere else at an output position.

Figur 3.2.1 illustrates the literal dependency graph for the second clause of perm mentioned in example 1.2, which is

p_2: perm(L,[H|T]) ← append^2(V,[H|U],L), append^1(V,U,W), perm(W,T).

The different modes by which append is used have been differentiated by superscripts. Please note that this graph is full.

A moded program is *well-moded* if the following holds:

- The dependency graph for every clause $A \leftarrow B_1,\ldots,B_n$ is full and defines a partial order '$<_l$' on its nodes (i. e. G_c is acyclic).
- If $A\leftarrow$ is a unit clause and σ is a substitution such that for all $v \in in(A)$ vσ is ground, then wσ is ground as well for all $w \in out(A)$.
- Let $\leftarrow B_1,\ldots,B_n$ be the goal clause. If B_i is minimal with regard to the partial order implied by G_c, then B_i is ground on all its input positions.
- If $B_i <_l B_j$, then $i \leq j$, i.e., the textual order of the literals in a clause is coherent with the partial order '$<_l$'.

The evaluation of the query of a given program is said to be *data driven* if at any resolution step the literal called is ground on all its input positions.

The following theorem is due to Dembinski and Maluszynski:

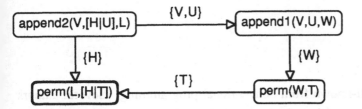

3.2.1 EXAMPLE: *Literal Dependency Graph for the second clause of perm*

3.2.2 THEOREM: *Data Driven Program Evaluation*

Evaluation of the query of a well-moded program is data driven under Prolog's standard search procedure. ∎

PROOF: See [DEM85].

For the *append*-procedure given in example 1.1 there are two modes which make this program well-moded, namely *mode append(+,+,-)* for concatenation and *mode append(-,-,+)* for splitting. It is implicitly understood that other modes such as *mode append(+,+,+)* are subsumed by those. The property of well-modedness as defined above only allows one mode for each predicate. This is no real restriction since it can easily be achieved by renaming. In the *perm*-procedure append is used in both modes. Appropriate modes for *perm* would be *perm(+,-)* and *perm(-,+)*. The *perm*-procedure in example 1.2 is well-moded only for the first mode, while for the second one the literals in the body of p_2 have to be reordered :

p'_2: perm(L,[H|T]) ← perm(W,T), append²(V,U,W), append¹(V,[H|U],L).

As illustrated above, the *perm*-program in its original version terminates in the first mode, while in the second mode it loops after the first answer. With p_2 replaced by p_2' *perm* terminates with the second mode, while it loops with the first mode after giving all answers. This example illustrates the fact that checking a program for well-modedness or - if possible - achieving this property by renaming of predicates and subgoal reordering can contribute to the elimination of unwanted loops.

This does not imply that mode declarations are to be supplied by the programmer. The problem of automatic generation of mode declarations has been studied - often in the context of abstract interpretation - by many authors, including for instance [MEL87] and [DEW88].

3.3 Types

The concept of types is well-known from conventional programming. Several authors have investigated the problem of introducing types in logic programming languages. Standard Prolog compilers do not offer type checking. On the other hand there are several built-in predicates and functions where only certain terms are allowed to be arguments. While flexibility can ease the burden of programming, lack of type checking makes it more difficult to find bugs.

Although there are no explicit type declarations, a great deal of data structure or type information is implicit in a Prolog program. Since (pure) Prolog can be regarded as a specification language, it is reasonable from a problem solving point of view to think of Prolog programs as specifying types as well as semantics. In this vein several authors have proposed techniques for automatic derivation of types.

Other authors have shown that explicit type informations can be used to structure the search space of certain queries and thus reach significant optimization.

We discuss the concept of types here because we are interested in the notion of *reflexive constructors*, which will be given at the end of this paragraph. The dot, for instance, is the reflexive constructor for lists. This notion will be used in 3.4 for the definition of a norm for terms which is based on a type concept.

From the point of view of logic introducing types can be justified by considering a *many-sorted* or *typed logic theory*. In such a theory variables, constants, function symbols, predicates and quantifiers are all typed. Variables and constants have types such as τ. Predicate symbols have types of the form $\tau_1 x...x\tau_n$, and function symbols have types of the form $\tau_1 x...x\tau_n \to \tau$. If f has type $\tau_1 x...x\tau_n \to \tau$ we say f has range type τ. For each type τ there is a universal quantifier $\forall_\tau$ and an existential quantifier $\exists_\tau$.

A term of type τ is inductively defined as follows:

- A variable of type τ is a term of type τ.
- A constant of type τ is a term of type τ.
- If f is an n-ary function symbol of type $\tau_1 x...x\tau_n \to \tau$ and for $i = 1,...,n$ t_i is a term of type τ_i then $f(t_1, ... ,t_n)$ is a term of type τ.

A typed well-formed formula is defined as follows:

- If p is an n-ary predicate symbol of type $\tau_1 x \ldots x \tau_n$ and each t_i is a term of type τ_i then $p(t_1, \ldots, t_n)$ is a typed atomic formula.
- If F and G are typed formulas, then so are $\neg F$, $F \wedge G$, $F \vee G$, $F \rightarrow G$ and $F \leftrightarrow P$.
- If F is a typed formula and x is a variable of type τ, then $\forall_\tau x$ F and $\exists_\tau x$ F are typed formulas.

The notions of interpretation and model, validity and satisfiability can be transfered from the untyped to the typed case in a rather straightforward way. Details can be found in [END72].

From a pragmatic point of view it is quite important that the programmer (or the type inference system) has sufficient flexibility in specifying the types of terms. Therefore, in the context of logic programming, usually *polymorphic type concepts* have been proposed.

The following definitions are taken from Horiuchi and Kanamori ([HOK87]). The latter propose to augment a Prolog program by a special *type construct* to seperate clauses defining types from program clauses defining procedures in the normal sense, e.g.,

type
    list([]).
    list([X|L]) ← list(L).
end.

'**type**' defines unary *type predicates* by definite clauses. The head of such a clause takes a term specifying a data structure as its argument. This term is either a constant b, called a bottom element, or a structured term of the form $f(t_1, \ldots, t_n)$ where f is called a *constructor*. The body consists of literals starting with type predicates giving type conditions on proper subterms of the argument of the head of the clause. Note that type predicates may be defined recursively. However, mutual recursion is disallowed.

Let τ be a type predicate. The set of all terms t such that $\tau(t)$ succeeds is called the type of τ and is denoted by $\underline{\tau}$. Note that terms in $\underline{\tau}$ are not necessarily ground.

Suppose that there are k type predicates $\tau_1,...,\tau_k$, defined by type constructs such that $\underline{\tau}_1,...,\underline{\tau}_k$ are disjoint modulo variable renaming. A type is one of the following k+2 sets of terms:

<u>any</u> : the set of all terms,

$\underline{\tau}_1$: the set of all terms satisfying the definition of τ_1

...

$\underline{\tau}_k$: the set of all terms satisfying the definition of τ_k

Ø : the empty set.

The *monomorphic* notion of types given so far can be extended to a polymorphic one, e.g.,

type

list$<\tau>$([]).

list$<\tau>$([X|L]) ← τ(X), list$<\tau>$(L).

end.

Thus list$<\tau>$ specifies a polymorphic type list, the elements of which are of type τ. In general, *polymorphic types* are introduced as follows:

type

p$<\tau_1,...,\tau_k>$(b$_1$).

...

p$<\tau_1,...,\tau_k>$(b$_m$).

p$<\tau_1,...,\tau_k>$(c$_1$(X$_{11}$,X$_{12}$,...,X$_{1n_1}$))← p$_{11}$(X$_{11}$),p$_{12}$(X$_{12}$),...,p$_{1n_1}$(X$_{1n_1}$).

...

p$<\tau_1,...,\tau_k>$(c$_h$(X$_{h1}$,X$_{h2}$,...,X$_{hn_h}$))← p$_{h1}$(X$_{h1}$),p$_{h2}$(X$_{h2}$),...,p$_{hn_h}$(X$_{hn_h}$).

end.

where p is a new polymorphic type predicate, the b$_i$ are new constants called bottom elements, c$_i$ are new function symbols called constructors and the p$_{ij}$ are type predicates of arbitrary polymorphic or monomorphic types or type parameters τ_i. Again we exclude mutual recursion.

Having two levels of paramaters this is, strictly speaking, a type definition scheme rather than a type definition.

A *type definition* is obtained from $p<\tau_1,...,\tau_k>$ by substituting type predicates $u_1,...,u_k$ for the parameters $\tau_1,...,\tau_k$. It is called an instance of $p<\tau_1,...,\tau_k>$ and is denoted by $p<u_1,...,u_k>$. The parameter τ_i is called a type parameter.

As Horiuchi and Kanamori show, such type definitions can be automatically inferred from a Prolog program using techniques of abstract interpretation (see [ABH87]) and OLDT resolution (see [TAS86]). For a detailed discussion of this topic, which is beyond the scope of this book, the reader is referred to [HOK87].

In this context of automating termination proofs we are interested in the type concept because of the close resemblance between recursively defined procedures and recursive data structures. We consider type definitions as a means of making explicit what is implicit in a program. We are especially interested to know which constructors are used to construct a term of a given type recursively. An answer can be given with the help of the notion of reflexive constructors, which goes back to Milner, Morrris and Newey [MMN75] and Aubin [AUB79].

Let τ be a type and

$$\tau(f(t_1,...,t_i,...,t_n)) \leftarrow ...\tau(t_i)...$$

a clause in the definition of τ. Then f is called *reflexive function symbol* or *reflexive constructor* for τ.

We will make further use of this notion in the next paragraph.

3.4 Partial Orderings and Predicate Inequalities

The basic techniques for proving the termination of recursion involve the identification of well-founded orderings. In this section we discuss partial, well-founded orderings on terms. For a detailed discussion of this topic we refer the reader to the survey of Dershowitz [DER87]. In this paragraph we further introduce the notions of linear norms and linear predicate inequalities. In chapter 7 we will show how to derive linear inequalities.

A *partially ordered set* $(S, >)$ consists of a set S and a transitive and irreflexive binary relation $>$ defined on elements on S.

A partially ordered set is said to be *totally ordered*, if for any two distinct elements s and s' either s > s' or s' > s. For example, both the set **Z** of integers and the set **N** of natural numbers are totally ordered by the 'strictly-greater-than'-relation. The set P(**Z**) of all subsets of the integers is partially ordered by the superset relation $\supseteq$.

An *extension* of a partial ordering > on S is a second partial ordering >' on S such that s > t implies s >' t for all s, t ∈ S, a *restriction* of > is a partial ordering >" such that s >" t implies s > t for all s, t ∈ S.

A partial ordering on terms > is said to be *well-founded* if it admits no infinite descending sequences $s_1 > s_2 > s_3 > ...$ of elements of S. Thus the 'strictly-greater-than'-relation is a well-founded ordering on **N**, since no sequence can descend beyond 0, but it is not well-founded on **Z**, since - 1 > -2 ... is an infinite descending sequence.

3.4.1 DEFINITION: *Simplification Ordering*

A partial ordering > on a set of terms T is called a *simplification ordering** if the following properties hold:

1) t > t' implies f(...t...) > f(...t'...)   *(replacement property)*
2) f(...t...) > t   *(subterm property)*
3) t > t' implies tσ > t'σ   *(stability under substitution)*

for all terms t, t' ∈ T and all substitutions σ. ∎

Simplification orderings are well-founded (see [DER87]).

Partial orderings on elements induce partial orderings on tuples. An n-tuple $(t_1,...,t_n)$ with $t_i \in T$ is *lexicographically* greater than another such tuple $(t_1',...,t_n')$ if $t_i > t_i'$ for some i ∈ {1,...,n} while $t_j = t_j'$ for all j < i. Here '>' refers to the partial ordering on T. If '>' is well-founded, then its lexicographic extension '$>^x$' is well-founded as well.

Partial orderings can also be extended to multisets. A *multiset* is an unordered collection of elements in which elements may appear more than once. If S is a set, M(S) denotes the set of all finite multisets with elements taken from S.

---

* Note that we assume that function symbols have a *fixed arity*. [DER87] also demands the *deletion property* f(...t...) > f(... ...) to handle function symbols with indefinite arity.

3.4.2 DEFINITION: *Multiset Ordering*

Let $(S,>)$ be a partially-ordered set. The multiset ordering $\gg$ on $M(S)$ is defined as follows:

$$M \gg M^* \iff \text{for some } X, Y \in M(S) \text{ where } \emptyset \neq X \subseteq M,$$
$$M^* = (M - X) \cup Y \text{ and } (\forall y \in Y)(\exists x \in X) \; x > y. \; \blacksquare$$

According to this ordering an element of a multiset can be replaced by any finite number of elements that are smaller with respect to '$>$'. Here is an example taking multisets of natural numbers: $\{2,3\} \gg \{1,1,3\}$. In this example we have $X = \{2\}$ and $Y = \{1,1\}$. Another example will be found in 8.5 where we give a well-founded ordering on multisets of literals in order to prove termination of a special unfolding strategy.

Dershowitz and Manna showed that $\gg$ is well-founded iff $>$ is well founded [DEM79].

Multiset orderings are also used in the recursive path ordering (RPO) which has been proposed by Dershowitz in [DER82]. RPO is a prominent example of a simplification ordering. We mention it here because such an ordering can also be used, albeit only in special cases, in order to generate termination proofs for logic programs. Such cases will be identified in 4.4 *(structural recursion)*.

3.4.3 DEFINITION: *Recursive Path Ordering (RPO)*

Let $>$ be a partial ordering, called a precedence, on a set of function symbols F. The recursive path ordering $>^*$ on the set $T(F)$ of terms over F is defined recursively as follows:

$$s >^* t \iff$$

either

(1) $s = f(s_1,...,s_m), \quad t = g(t_1,...,t_n)$

and (1a) $f = g$ and $\{s_1,...,s_m\}$ $\gg^*$ $\{t_1,...,t_n\}$ or

(1b) $f > g$ and $\{s\}$ $\gg^*$ $\{t_1,...,t_n\}$ or

(1c) $f \not> g$ and $\{s_1,...,s_m\}$ $\geqslant^*$ $\{t\}$

or

(2) $t = v \in vars(s)$ and $v \neq s$.

Here $\gg^*$ is the multiset ordering induced by $>^*$ and $\geq^*$ means $\gg^*$ or $=$. Two terms shall be considered equal if they are the same except for permutations among subterms.
∎

We use RPO as an example to illustrate the fact that the rule of distributivity fits into a terminating term rewriting system. We have $F = \{'+','*'\}$ and assume '*' > '+' as a precedence among the symbols of F. We show

(I) $X * (Y + Z) >^* (X * Y) + (X * Z)$.

Since '*' > '+', according to (1b) we have to show

(II) $X * (Y + Z) >^* X * Y$ and
(III) $X * (Y + Z) >^* X * Z$.

We discuss only (II). Since both of the terms $X * (Y + Z)$ and $X * Y$ have the same outermost functor, (1a) has to be applied. We have to show that

(IV) $\{X, Y+Z\} \gg^* \{X, Y\}$.

Since the variable 'Y' occurs in the term 'Y + Z' and 'Y' ≠ 'Y + Z', (IV) is true according to (2).

The recursive path ordering can be enhanced by a lexicographic component which modifies (1a). In order to show that

$s = f(s_1,...,s_m) >^* f(t_1,...,t_m)$, where $s >^* t_i$ for $i = 1,...,m$,

the tuples $(s_1,...,s_m)$ and $(t_1,...,t_m)$ are compared lexicographically instead of comparing them as multisets. Lexicographic comparison can be made from left to right, from right to left or in any fixed order. The specific way of comparing arguments is referred to as the *status* of a function symbol [BAC88]. An example where this modification of RPO is useful is associativity:

(V) $(X * Y) * Z >^* X * (Y * Z)$.

Whereas the multiset $\{(X * Y), Z\}$ is not bigger than $\{(Y * Z), X\}$, lexicographic comparison of the corresponding tuples is possible:

(VI) $((X * Y), Z) >^x (X, (Y * Z))$

since $X * Y >^* X$. We will come back to this example in 4.5 *(bounded recursion)*.

In our context there are two problems with RPO. The first problem is that a precedence among the function symbols has to be given. If one does not want to have the user to specify such a precedence, all possible orderings may have to be checked. This can be quite expensive. Even more important is the fact that RPO can rarely be applied if there are local variables. The problem of local variables will be discussed at length in chapter 5.

Our approach, which is based on linear predicate inequalities, needs the notion of linear norms.

3.4.4 DEFINITION: *Term Norms*

For a set T of terms a *norm* is a mapping $| \ldots |: T \to N$. We say that $| t |$ is the *weight* of t (w. r. t. $| \ldots |$). The restriction of $| \ldots |$ to ground terms is denoted by $| \ldots |^g$. ∎

3.4.5 DEFINITION: *Linear Term Norms*

A norm $| \ldots |$ for T is said to be *linear* if for each $t \in T$ and each instantiation σ for t

$$| t\sigma | = | t | + \sum_{i=1}^{n} | v_i\sigma |$$

holds, where $\{v_1, \ldots, v_n\}$ is the multiset of variable occurrences in t. For a linear norm *with zero-terms* there exists a term t such that $| t | = 0$. ∎

A linear norm can be defined by the giving of function symbol weights.

3.4.6 DEFINITION: *Term Norms induced by Function Symbol Weights*

Let F be the set of function symbols occurring in a set of terms T. We say that a norm $| \ldots |$ on terms is *induced by function symbol weights*, if the following holds:

$| v |$	$= 0$	if v is a variable symbol
$| c |$	$= \Phi(c)$	if c is a 0-ary function symbol
$| f(t_1, \ldots, t_n) |$	$= \Phi(f) + \sum_{i=1}^{n} | t_i |$	if f is an n-ary function symbol with $n > 0$

for the mapping $\Phi: F \to N$ which defines the function symbol weights.

3.4.7 Proposition: *Linear Term Norms*

A term norm induced by function symbol weights is linear.

PROOF: The proof is by induction on term structure. Let t be a term and σ a substitution which makes t ground. If $t = v$ is a variable, $|v| = 0$ implies $|v\sigma| = |v| + |v\sigma|$. If $t = c$ is a constant, $|c\sigma| = |c|$. Now let us assume that $t = f(t_1,...,t_n)$. Assume that for $1 \le i \le n$ V_i is the multiset of variable occurrences in t_i. By the induction assumption we have

$$|t_i\sigma| \quad = \quad |t_i| + \sum_{v \in V_i} |v\sigma|$$

for all i, and thus

$$|f(t_1,...,t_n)\sigma| \quad = \quad \Phi(f) + \sum_{i=1}^{n} \sum_{v \in V_i} (|t_i| + |v\sigma|)$$

$$= \quad |f(t_1,...,t_n)| + \sum_{v \in V} |v\sigma|$$

where V is the multiset of variable occurrences in $f(t_1,...,t_n)$, i.e., the multiset-union of all the V_i. ∎

Let $\Phi(c)$ be zero for all constants c. If $\Phi(f) = n$ for all n-ary function symbols f, then the norm $|...|_n$ induced by Φ will be called *n-norm*. If $\Phi(f) = 1$ for all function symbols f with arity greater zero, then the norm $|...|_1$ induced by Φ will be called *1-norm*.

Another interesting norm is the type norm.

3.4.8 DEFINITION: *The type norm*

This norm assumes that type definitions are given. Let τ be a type. Then we have

$$|c|_\tau \qquad\qquad = 0 \qquad\qquad \text{if c is a variable or a constant.}$$

$$|f(t_1, ..., t_n)|_\tau = 1 + \sum_{i=1}^{n} |t_i|_\tau \qquad \text{if f is a reflexive constructor for } \tau$$

$$|f(t_1, ..., t_n)|_\tau = \qquad \sum_{i=1}^{n} |t_i|_\tau \qquad \text{otherwise.}$$

This norm counts the number of occurrences of reflexive constructors for τ in a given term (which is not necessarily of type τ). Since the type norm is induced by function symbol weights it is linear.

3.4.9 EXAMPLE: *Several norms applied to [a,f(a)]*

Consider the term [a,f(a)] which is a shorthand notation for .(a, .(f(a),nil)). We have

$\mid [a,f(a)] \mid_1$	$= 3$	for the 1-norm,
$\mid [a,f(a)] \mid_n$	$= 5$	for the n-norm,
$\mid [a,f(a)] \mid_\tau$	$= 2$	for the type norm and $\tau = $ type list(any).

Another norm, which is interesting for historical reasons, is the Knuth-Bendix-norm.

3.4.10 DEFINITION: *Knuth-Bendix norm*

The *Knuth-Bendix norm* is defined as follows:

$\mid c \mid_{KB}$	$= \#_c$	if c is a 0-ary function symbol,
$\mid v \mid_{KB}$	$= m$	if v is a variable,

$$\mid f(t_1,...,t_n) \mid_{KB} = \#_f + \sum_{i=1}^{n} \mid t_i \mid_{KB} \quad \text{if f is a n-ary function symbol, for n} > 0.$$

where # assigns a positive integer to each 0-ary function symbol and a nonnegative integer to each other function symbol occurring in a term t in T and m is the minimum weight for a 0-ary function symbol. This norm goes back to [KNB70]. ∎

The Knuth-Bendix-norm is not linear, since $\mid v\sigma \mid_{KB} = \mid v \mid_{KB} + \mid v\sigma \mid_{KB}$ does not necessarily hold. There is, however, a weaker property which is satisfied.

We say a term norm $\mid ... \mid$ *respects instantiations* if, for every term t with variable occurrences $\{v_1,...,v_n\}$ and for every instantiation θ, we have

$$\mid t\theta \mid \geq \sum_{i=1}^{n} \mid v_i\theta \mid.$$

Obviously, a linear norm respects instantiations.

3.4.11 PROPOSITION: *The Knuth-Bendix norm respects instantiations.*

PROOF: Immediately by induction on the structure of terms. ∎

A norm | ... | on a set of terms T induces a partial ordering > in the following way:

$$| t | > | t' | :\Leftrightarrow   t > t'.$$

Since | ... | is a mapping from terms to N, > is well-founded.

We next introduce the notion of linear predicate inequalities. This notion has some relation to what has been called *'interargument inequality'* by Ullman and van Gelder in [ULG88]. Our format, however, is more general from the beginning, thus we have to be more careful with syntactic details. We start with a definition which specifies the format of linear inequalities. Sometimes we will be only interested in knowing which arguments are related by a special inequality. For this aim it is sufficient to know the format of an inequality. What it means for an inequality to be valid is defined in 3.4.13.

3.4.12 DEFINITION: *Linear Predicate Inequalities*

Let p be an n-ary predicate in a program P, and let I and J be disjoint sets of indices such that $I \cup J \subseteq \{1,...,n\}$. For $i \in I \cup J$ p_i is called an argument designator for p. A *linear predicate inequality* LI_p for p has the form

$$\sum_{i \in I} p_i + c \geq \sum_{j \in J} p_j$$

where $c \in Z \cup \{\gamma, \infty\}$. $I = Pos_{in}(LI_p)$ and $J = Pos_{out}(LI_p)$ are the sets of in- resp. out-positions of p (w.r.t. LI_p), $c = o(LI_p)$ is called the *offset* of LI_p. LI_p is called *symbolic*, if $o(LI_p) = \gamma$. '∞' will be used with its standard meaning. If I and J are both singletons, LI_p is called binary.

We say that LI_p is *stronger* than another inequality LI_p' for the same predicate p if

- $Pos_{in}(LI_p) \subseteq Pos_{in}(LI_p')$ and
- $Pos_{out}(LI_p) \supseteq Pos_{out}(LI_p')$ and
- $o(LI_p) \in Z$, $o(LI_p') \in Z$ and $o(LI_p) \leq o(LI_p')$
  or $o(LI_p)$ is an integer and $o(LI_p')$ is '∞'.

LI_p is *strictly stronger* than LI_p' if it is stronger and not equal to LI_p'. ∎

Naming suggests that in- and out-positions (w.r.t. *inequalities*) are related to input- resp. output-positions (w.r.t. *modes*). Although this will be the case quite often in termination proofs, it should be kept in mind that modes and inequalities are two independent concepts. There is an important difference between these concepts: while modes refer to the *operational* semantics of a program, valid linear inequalities refer to the *declarative* semantics of a program, as the following definition makes it clear. A linear norm |...| will be implicitly assumed in the following.

3.4.13 DEFINITION: *Valid Linear Predicate Inequalities*

The predicate inequality

$$\sum_{i \in I} p_i + c \geq \sum_{j \in J} p_j$$

is *valid* for a predicate p in a program P (or p satisfies this inequality), if either $c = \infty$ or for every atom $p(t_1,...,t_n)$ in the minimal Herbrand model of P the following inequality holds:

$$\sum_{i \in I} |t_i| + c \geq \sum_{j \in J} |t_j|$$

Valid linear predicate inequalities characterize *ground* atomic formulas which are elements of the minimal Herbrand model of a program. They can be used to relate terms occurring in such atoms. We next discuss how correct answer substitutions for one-literal goals, such as ← append(X,Y,Z), can be characterized by valid inequalities. Compound goals will be considered in chapter 6. First we need some more technical notations.

3.4.14 DEFINITION *In- and Out-Variables*

Let a predicate p, an inequality LI_p for p, and a p-literal L be given.

* In(L, LI_p) is the multiset of variable occurrences on the in-positions of L.
* Out(L, LI_p) is the multiset of variable occurrences on the out-positions of L.

3.4.15 Proposition: *Offsets of Literals*

Let a predicate p, an inequality LI_p for p, and $L = p(t_1,...,t_n)$ be given. I and J are the in- resp. out-positions of p. Again a linear norm $|...|$ is implicitly assumed. We then define

- $F_{in}(L,LI_p) \quad = \quad \sum_{i \in I} |t_i|$

- $F_{out}(L,LI_p) \quad = \quad \sum_{j \in J} |t_j|$

- $F(L,LI_p) \quad = \quad F_{in}(L,LI_p) - F_{out}(L,LI_p) + o(LI_p).$

$F(L,LI_p)$ is called the *offset* of L.

3.4.16 PROPOSITION: *Ground Answer Substitutions*

Let LI_p be a valid linear inequality for p in P with offset c having I and J as in- resp. out-positions. Let σ be a ground answer substitution for $\leftarrow L$, where $L = p(t_1,...,t_n)$. Let V and W be the multisets of variable occurrences on the in- resp. out-positions of L. Then the following inequality holds:

$$\sum_{v \in V} |v\sigma| + F(L) \geq \sum_{w \in W} |w\sigma|.$$

PROOF: Since σ is a correct answer, validity of LI_p implies

$$\sum_{i \in I} |t_i\sigma| + c \geq \sum_{j \in J} |t_j\sigma|.$$

Since $|...|$ is linear we get

$$\sum_{v \in V} |v\sigma| + \sum_{i \in I} |t_i| + c \geq \sum_{w \in W} |w\sigma| + \sum_{j \in J} |t_j|.$$

Now by 2.5

$$F(L) = \sum_{i \in I} |t_i| - \sum_{j \in J} |t_j| + c$$

which proves the claim.

In conclusion we give an example illustrating the notions defined above.

3.4.17 EXAMPLE: *Linear inequality for append*

Consider the append-predicate defined in example 1.1. A linear inequality for append is

$\quad$ LI_{append}: $append_1 + append_2 \geq append_3$.

For the 1-norm $|...|_1$ this inequality is valid. We now consider the literal $\leftarrow A$ with $A = append([H_1|L_1],L_2,L_3)$. We have $F_{in}(A) = |[H_1|L_1]| + |L_2| = 1$, $F_{out}(A) = |L_3| = 0$, $o(LI_{append}) = 0$ and thus $F(A) = 1$. With 3.4.16 we have

$\quad$ $|H_1\sigma|_1 + |L_1\sigma|_1 + |L_2\sigma|_1 + 1 \geq |L_3\sigma|_1$

for every ground answer substitution σ for $\leftarrow A$. ∎

If we consider a goal $G = \leftarrow A$, $A = p(t_1,...,t_n)$, a program P and a correct answer substitution θ for G, we cannot be sure that $A\theta$ is ground. We know, however, that all ground instances of $A\theta$ are in the minimal Herbrand model M_P of P. If we have a valid linear inequality LI_P for p an interesting question is whether LI_P can also be used to characterize the nonground case such that the following inequality holds:

$$(+) \quad \sum_{i \in I} |t_i\theta| + o(LI_P) \geq \sum_{j \in J} |t_j\theta|.$$

This inequality does not hold in general, however, as the following example shows:

Let the program P consist of the unit clauses $p(X)$ and $q(a)$ and let $|...|$ be the linear norm which maps the term a to 1, while variables are mapped to zero. Note that $HU_P = \{a\}$ and $M_P = \{p(a),q(a)\}$. The following inequality is valid: $p_1 - 1 \geq 0$. The empty substitution $\{\}$ is a correct answer for the goal $\leftarrow p(X)$. $|X| - 1 \geq 0$, however, does not hold, since $|X| = 0$.

The problem in the last example is that variables are mapped to zero, while all non-variable terms are mapped to numbers greater than 0. If linear norms with zero-terms are considered, inequality (+) holds, as the following proposition shows.

3.4.18 PROPOSITION: *Characterization of logical consequences*

Let LI_p be a valid linear inequality for p in P with offset c having I and J as in- resp. out-positions. Let σ be a correct answer substitution for $\leftarrow L$, where $L\sigma = p(t_1,\ldots,t_n)$. Then the following inequality holds:

$$(*) \qquad \sum_{i\in I}|t_i| + c \geq \sum_{j\in J}|t_j| .$$

PROOF: Let v be a variable. We first note that $|\ldots|$ being a linear norm implies that $|v\sigma| = |v| + |v\sigma|$ and thus $|v| = 0$. Let t be a term with $|t| = 0$, $V = \{v_1,\ldots,v_n\}$ be the set of variables occurring in $L\sigma$ and $\theta = \{v_1/t,\ldots,v_n/t\}$. Since LI_P is valid and $L\sigma\theta$ is in M_P, we have:

$$(**) \qquad \sum_{i\in I}|t_i\theta| + c \geq \sum_{j\in J}|t_j\theta| .$$

Since for all $v \in V$ $|v| = |t| = 0$, $(**)$ implies $(*)$. ∎

An immediate consequence is the following generalization of proposition 3.4.16:

3.4.19 PROPOSITION: *Correct Answer Substitutions*

Let $|\ldots|$ be a linear norm with zero-terms and LI_p be a valid linear inequality for p in P with offset c having I and J as in- resp. out-positions. Let θ be a *correct* (but not necessarily ground) answer substitution for $\leftarrow L$, where $L = p(t_1,\ldots,t_n)$. Let V and W be the multisets of variable occurrences on the in- resp. out-positions of L. Then the following inequality holds:

$$\sum_{v\in V}|v\theta| + F(L) \geq \sum_{w\in W}|w\theta| .$$

3.5 Unfolding

In logic programming unfolding techniques are widely used in the context of *partial evaluation*. Partial evaluation is an optimization technique dating back to Kleenes s-m-n theorem [KLE52]. Partial evaluation is applied in order to specialize a general program to a special efficient program using information about the runtime environment, especially the input data. The basic principle of partial evaluation is to evaluate parts of a program which do have enough input data and to keep them as they are if the parts do not have enough data. In functional languages concrete values of variables are usually necessary in order to evaluate expressions. Otherwise special schemes like lazy evaluation are required. In the context of logic programming computation is based on unification, thus no special evaluation scheme is required for partial evaluation. This advantage, which has been identified by several authors (see for instance [TAF86]), is important for our purposes.

In our context of termination we do not have optimization in mind. Instead we are interested in program analysis, and we apply program transformations because a transformed program can often be better analyzed than the original one. Moreover, with regard to termination, a transformed program can also have a better operational behaviour than the original one, while its declarative semantic is the same.

Unfolding is an important part of partial evaluation techniques. Essentially, it consists of replacing an atom A in the body of a clause with the body of another clause whose head H is unifiable with A, and applying the most general unifier of H and A to the result. No input is needed for this transformation.

With regard to unfolding two important questions have to be discussed:

a)   under which conditions does such a program transformation preserve the declarative semantics of a program?

b)   how can the process of program transformation specified by the unfolding technique be guided? How can the termination of this process be guaranteed?

To answer the first question we will sum up some results of Lloyd and Sheperdson (see [LLS87]). For the second question we will give an answer of our own in chapter 8.

3.5.1 DEFINITION: *Resultant*

Let $\Pi = (P,G)$ be a queried program, where the query G consists of the single atom Q. Let $G_0 = G$, $G_1,\ldots,G_n$ be an SLDNF-derivation of Π, where the sequence of substitutions is $\theta_1, \theta_2,\ldots,\theta_n$ and G_n is $\leftarrow Q_n$. Then we say that the derivation has length n with computed answer $\theta = \theta_1\ldots\theta_n$ and *resultant* $Q\theta \leftarrow Q_n$. (If n=0, the resultant is $Q \leftarrow Q$.) ∎

3.5.2 DEFINITION: *Unfolding*

Let $\Pi = (P,G)$ be a queried program, where the query G consists of the single atom A, and T be an partial SLDNF-tree for Π. Let $G_1,...,G_r$ be (non-root) goals in T chosen so that each non-failing branch of T contains exactly one of them. Let R_i (i=1,...,r) be the resultants of the derivation of G_i from G given by the branch leading to G_i. Then the set of clauses $R_1,...,R_r$ is called an unfolding of A in P.

An *unfolding of Π* w.r.t. A is a program obtained from P by replacing the set of clauses in P whose head contains the predicate symbol of A (called the unfolded predicate) by an unfolding of A in P. ■

3.5.3 EXAMPLE: *Unfolding of 'grandparent' in the Family-program*

Consider the following program representing parts of the Holy Family of the ancient Greeks:

    parent(zeus,ares).
    parent(ares,harmonia).
    parent(harmonia,semele).
    grandparent(X,Z) ← parent(X,Y),parent(Y,Z).

Let T be the SLD-tree for the goal *grandparent(X,Z)* as shown above. Let T' be the subtree of T containing the derivations of length one. T' is a partial SLD-tree. The resultants we get are:

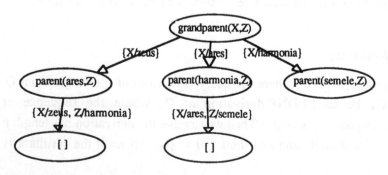

SLD-tree *for grandparent(X,Z)*

grandparent(zeus,Z)   ← parent(ares,Z).
grandparent(ares,Z)   ← parent(harmonia,Z).
grandparent(harmonia,Z) ← parent(semele,Z).

The resultants we get from T are:

grandparent(zeus,harmonia).
grandparent(ares,semele).

Both of these sets can safely replace the original clause for grandparent without changing the semantics of the original program.

If, however, we consider an unfolding HF' of the original program HF with regard to the goal ←grandparent(zeus,X), completeness is lost. For the goal 'grandparent(ares,X)' we do not get any answer, although X = semele is a correct answer with regard to HF. The reason is that this new goal is not an instance of the atom grandparent(zeus,X) which was unfolded. This motivates the following definition.

3.5.4 DEFINITION: *A-closed formulas*

Let S be a set of first order formulas and A an atom. We say that S is *A-closed* if each atom in S containing a predicate symbol occurring in A is an instance of A.

3.5.5 THEOREM: *Completeness of Unfolding*

Let P be a logic program, G a goal, A an atom and P' an unfolding of P w.r.t. A using SLD-trees such that P' ∪ {G} is A-closed. Then the following holds:

- P' ∪ {G} has an SLD-refutation with computed answer θ if P ∪ {G} does.
- P' ∪ {G} has a finitely failed SLD-tree if P ∪ {G} does.

PROOF: See [LLS87].

The following example shows that with regard to termination the operational behaviour of a program can in fact be substantially improved by unfolding.

3.5.6 EXAMPLE: *Single element list.*

$p(X) \leftarrow l(X), q(X).$
$q([A]).$
$r(1).$
$l([]).$
$l([H|T]) \leftarrow r(H), l(T).$

Consider an unfolding of this program w.r.t. $p(X)$, where only $q(X)$ is reduced. The clause for p can then be replaced by the following one:

$p([A]) \leftarrow l([A]).$

If we now consider an SLD-tree for $p(Z)$ w.r.t. the original program, we see that it is infinite, while for the unfolding the SLD-tree is finite.

Chapter 4

TERMINATING LOGIC PROGRAMS

Aims of this chapter are a theoretical characterization of terminating queries and a syntactic characterization of procedures which can be regarded as primitive (or structural) recursive.

When termination of programs is considered, two different views can be taken. One view would say that a program terminates if it either fails finitely or produces at least one successful derivation. Following Vasak and Potter [VAP86], this property is called *existential termination*. Such a view may be reasonable from a problem solving point of view, where the question is whether an answer to a specified problem can be given. In the context of logic programming, such an approach to define termination has some disadvantages. Here it is important that the following conclusion is valid:

"Given that the two goals ←p and ←q *terminate*.
Then the goal ← p, q *terminates* as well."

If *"termination"* stands for *"existential termination"*, however, this conclusion is wrong, as the following example, discussed in [DAR81] and [NAI86], illustrates:

4.0.1 EXAMPLE: *Append3*

Consider the following definition of append3 :
    append3(A,B,C,D) ← append(A,B,E), append(E,C,D).
This procedure works well for joining lists. Evaluating the goal

    ← append3([f,r],[e],[d],D)

the interpreter will bind the local variable E to $[f,r,e]$ after a first successful call of $append([f,r],[e],E)$, and the call $append([f,r,e],[d],D)$ will then bind D to $[f,r,e,d]$ as expected. Backtracking will yield no further solutions. Problems, however, will arise if append3 is invoked in a different mode, for instance:

← append3(X,[e],[d],[f,r,e,d])

Here it is asked for a prefix list X of a list $[f,r,e,d]$ given the suffix lists $[e]$ and $[d]$.

The first call to append matches the first clause for append, binding X to $[]$. The second call to *append* fails. Retrying the first call to *append* twice results in binding X to a two element list, elements being unbound variables. With this binding the second call to *append* immediately succeeds. Further backtracking, however, results in the first *append* literal consecutively binding X to variable lists of increasing length, while the second *append* literal fails again and again.

What is important here is the following: Although evaluation of the goal ←*append(X,[e],Y)* gives a first solution after a finite number of steps, it may give rise to an infinite computation since this goal generates an *infinite* number of solutions. Generally, if we have

... generate(...X...), test(...X...) ...

where *'generate'* produces an infinite number of solutions, such that *'test'* fails for all of them, we have an infinite computation.

To cope with such a sort of problems, a stronger notion of termination is needed. Termination, as will be defined below, means that all derivations are finite. An interesting property of this notion, which has been called *universal termination* in [VAP86] is that while it is sensitive to the computation rule, clause selection (or clause ordering in Prolog) is irrelevant.

4.1 Proof Trees

In chapter 2 SLD-trees have been introduced as a means of describing the evaluation of a goal. A disadvantage of this model for our purpose here is that there is no obvious correspondence between the subgoals in the body of a clause and the selected subgoals in a branch of the SLD-tree. For the characterization of terminating queries, the notion of proof trees, introduced by Clark [CLA79], is a better device. The main advantage of this concept for our purpose is that recursion corresponds directly to branches of proof trees. The following definitions are adopted from [VAP86].

4.1.1 DEFINITION: *Proof Trees*

For a queried program $\Pi = (P,G)$, where G consists of the single atom A, a *proof tree* T satisfies the following conditions:

- the root node of T is an instance of A
- if S is a non leaf node with immediate descendants $R_1,...,R_k$, then the clause $S \leftarrow R_1,...,R_k$ is an instance of a clause in P.

A proof tree is *complete* if all leaf nodes are facts.

4.1.2 DEFINITION: *Successful derivations of limited depth*

- $suc_n(P) = \{ Q \mid Q$ is a (not necessarily ground) atom such that there is a complete proof tree of depth n at most with root Q$\}$
- $suc(P) = \{ Q \mid Q$ is a (not necessarily ground) atom such that there is a complete proof tree of finite depth with root Q$\}$. ■

4.1.3 PROPOSITION: *Suc(P) specifies the Least Fixpoint of P*

For the least fixpoint M_P of a program P we have:

$M_P = \{ Q\theta \mid Q \in suc(P)$ and θ is an instantiation for Q$\}$. ■

PROOF: see [CLA79].

4.1.4 DEFINITION: *Expansion of Proof Trees*

Let T be a proof tree for $\Pi = (P,G)$ and S a leaf atom of T (the selected atom). T' is derived by expanding T from S by one of the following transformations:

- In P there is a unit clause S' such that $S\theta = S'\theta$ and $T' = T\theta$.
- In P there is a clause $S' \leftarrow R_1,...,R_k$, $S\theta = S'\theta$, the atoms $R_1,...,R_k$ are added to T as immediate descendants of S, and θ is applied to all nodes of the tree.

A proof tree is completely expanded to depth n if there are no unexpanded nodes of depth $\leq$ n. ∎

4.1.5 DEFINITION: *Computation of a Proof tree w.r.t. a given rule*

As in chapter 2, a computation rule is a mapping from goals to single atoms. A finite proof tree T for $\Pi = (P,G)$, where G is the single atom Q, is computed according to a given computation rule if it is either

- the single node Q
- the expansion of a computed proof tree with an unexpanded node selected by the computation rule.

If the atom associated with the selected node is not unifiable with the head of any program clause, the computation fails. ∎

4.2 Terminating Queries

We now make precise what is meant by a terminating query. The idea is that a terminating query is one which has a finite number of derivations, all of which are finite.

4.2.1 DEFINITION: *Terminating Queries*

For a given program P we have

a) $Term_n(P) = \{Q \in HB_p \mid \forall\theta$, all computed proof trees for $(P,Q\theta)$ are of depth $\leq n\}$
b) $Term(P) = \{Q \in HB_p \mid \forall\theta$, all computed proof trees for $(P,Q\theta)$ are of a finitely
bounded depth$\}$
Term(P) is called the set of terminating queries of P. ∎

Note that

- $Term_n(P) \subseteq Term_{n+1}(P)$,

- $Term(P) = \bigcup_{n \in N} Term_n(P)$,

- $Term(P)$ is dependent on the computation rule,

- $Term(P)$ is closed under substitution.

Obviously, unsolvability of the halting problem implies that it is not decidable whether or not an arbitrary query is element of $Term(P)$. It is possible, however, to characterize $Term_n(P)$ for a given n. The following definitions characterize $Term_n(P)$ by its complement.

4.2.2 DEFINITION: $N_n(P)$ and $Co\text{-}N_n(P)$

$N_n(P)$ = $\{Q \in HB_P \mid \forall \theta$, there is a computed proof tree of depth $n+1$ with root $Q\theta\}$

$co\text{-}N_n(P)$ = $\{Q \in HB_P \mid Q$ is not unifiable with any element of $N_n(P)\}$ ∎

Thus if Q is in $co\text{-}N_n(P)$, its derivation, if any, has at most depth n.

4.2.3 DEFINITION: *Inductive Definition of* M_n

$M_0(P)$ = HB_P

$M_n(P)$ = $\{Q \in HB_P \mid \exists(Q \leftarrow R_1,...,R_k) \in P, \exists \theta, \exists i \in \{1...k\}$ such that $R_i\theta \in M_{n-1}(P) \wedge \{R_1,...,R_i\} \subseteq Suc_{n-1}(P) \cup M_{n-1}(P)\}$

$co\text{-}M_n(P)$ = $\{Q \in HB_P \mid Q$ is not unifiable with any element of $M_n(P)\}$

Note that $N_n(P)$ refers to any computation rule, while $M_n(P)$ refers to the standard computation rule of Prolog.

The following theorem is due to Vasak and Potter [VAP86]:

4.2.4 THEOREM: *Complementary Characterization of* $Term_n$

1) $Term_n(P) = co\text{-}N_n(P)$
2) $Term_n(P) = co\text{-}M_n(P)$

PROOF:

1) $Q \in \text{Term}_n(P)$ if $\forall \theta$

    all computed proof trees for $Q\theta$ are of depth $\leq n$ $\Leftrightarrow$

    no computed proof tree for $Q\theta$ is of depth $\geq n+1$ $\Leftrightarrow$

    $Q\theta \notin N_n(P)$ $\Leftrightarrow$

    $Q\theta \in \text{co-}N_n(P)$.

2) By always choosing the smallest possible i the definition of $M_n(P)$ can be rewritten in the following way:

$$M_n(P) = \{Q \in HB_P \mid \exists(Q \leftarrow R_1,...,R_k) \in P, \exists\, \theta, \exists\, i \in \{1,...,k\} \text{ such that}$$
$$R_i\theta \in M_{n-1}(P) \wedge \{R_1,...,R_{i-1}\} \subseteq \text{Suc}_{n-1}(P)\}.$$

Induction on n then shows that $M_n(P) = N_n(P)$. ∎

4.3 Recursive Loops

In the last section terminating queries were specified. If bounds on the depth of computation trees are considered, theorem 4.2.4 suggests a way to enumerate the set of terminating queries recursively. Unsolvability of the halting problem, however, implies that this set is not recursive. So what one can get at best is an approximative characterization of this set by sufficient criteria. To achieve this we next consider procedures which are assumed to be well moded. As stated in 3.2.2 this property guarantees that each literal, when called, is ground on all its input positions. This allows to approach the problem of termination with the help of well-founded orderings on *ground* terms.

We start with some more or less straightforward statements which give simple sufficient syntactic conditions for termination.

4.3.1 DEFINITION: *Terminating Procedures of well-moded programs*

A procedure π defining a predicate p of a well-moded program P is said to be terminating if each query $\leftarrow p(t_1,...,t_n)$ is terminating, whenever $p(t_1,...,t_n)$ is ground on all its input positions. We also say that the predicate p defined by that procedure is terminating. ∎

Note that in a well-moded program we assume that there is exactly one mode for each predicate.

4.3.2 PROPOSITION: *Nonrecursive programs always terminate*

Let P be a program and D_P its predicate dependency graph. If D_P is acyclic, then each predicate of P is terminating.

PROOF: Define a relation on atoms as follows:

$p(t_1,...,t_n) >_\alpha q(u_1,...,u_m)$ if $p \not\rightarrow q$.

Acyclity of D_p implies that $'>_\alpha'$ is a partial ordering. Since the set of predicates in P is finite, $>_\alpha$ is well-founded. For any proof tree w.r.t P we have $L >_\alpha L'$ if L' is son node of L. Let n be length of the longest path of D_P. Then we have $M_n(P) = \emptyset$. ∎

Note that the predicate dependency graph D_P of a program P is acyclic if and only if P has no recursion.

Since the number of different predicates in a given program is finite, an infinite path in a proof tree must contain infinitely many occurrences of the same predicate symbol. In the chapters 6 and 7 we will restrict attention to programs which are free of mutual recursion. For this programs we have that beyond a certain point successive nodes of an infinite branch must have the same predicate symbol. Such branches will be called recursive loops. We make this precise in the following.

4.3.3 DEFINITION: *Recursive Branches and Loops*

A branch $L_1,...,L_i,...$ of a L_0-rooted proof tree T is called recursive, if for some $i \geq 0$ all nodes L_j with $j \geq i$ are literals which have the same predicate symbol p. If this branch is infinite, it is called recursive loop for p.

4.3.4 PROPOSITION: *Recursive Loops and Direct Recursion*

For a queried program $\Pi = (P,G)$ such that P is free of mutual recursion and G is a single literal goal, each infinite proof tree has a recursive loop.

PROOF: By contradiction. If T is infinite, Königs infinity lemma [KNU73] implies that there is at least one infinite branch D. Assuming that D is not a recursive loop implies that there exist at least two predicates p and q with infinitely many successive occurrences. Thus we have $p \underset{\pi}{\not\to} q$ and $q \underset{\pi}{\not\to} p$ contradicting the assumption that P is free of mutual recursion. ∎

4.4 Structural and Primitive Recursion

The last proposition suggests a first straightforward, although rather restricted technique to prove termination of well-moded programs: Let a well-founded ordering '$>_t$' on ground terms be given. Take the subterm ordering as an example, where $t > t'$ if and only if t' is a proper subterm of t. Consider all recursive procedures. For each recursive procedure p consider all recursive clauses. For each recursive clause c_i, consider all recursive literals c_{ij} and compare them with c_{io}, the head of C_i. Let $<t_1,...,t_m>$ be the input terms of c_{io} and $<t_1',...,t_m'>$ the input terms of c_{ij}. Check if $<t_1,...,t_m>\theta >_t <t_1',...,t_m'>\theta$ for all instantiations θ. (This check is superflous, of course, if $>_t$ is stable under substitution.) If this is true there are no recursive loops for p.

We render this idea precise in the next definition.

4.4.1 DEFINITION: *Structural Recursive Procedures*

Let $\pi = \{C_1,...,C_m\}$ be a recursive procedure definition for an n-ary predicate p in a well-moded program P which has no mutual recursion, and let $>_t$ be any well-founded ordering on ground terms. The procedure π is said to be structural recursive if

∃   a set of input indices $I = \{i_1,...,i_k\} \subseteq \{1,...,n\}$ such that
∀   recursive clauses C_j with head $C_{j0} = p(t_1,...,t_n)$
∀   recursive literals C_{jr} in C_j with $C_{jr} = p(t_1',...,t_n')$

we have for all θ instantiating $t_{i1},...,t_{ik}$:

(i) $t_i\theta \geq_t t_i'\theta$ for all $j \in \{i_1,...,i_k\}$
(ii) $t_q\theta >_t t_q'\theta$ for some $q \in \{i_1,...,i_k\}$

We also say that the predicate p defined by π is structural recursive. ∎

Thus we call a procedure structurally recursive if one of a subset of the input arguments is guaranteed to decrease and none in this set increase in any recursive call. This notion of structural recursion corresponds to a concept proposed in the dissertation of Naish (see [NAI86]). The conditions (i) and (ii) could be generalized to a lexicographic ordering on input terms.

4.4.2 THEOREM: *Structural Recursion terminates*

If a procedure π for a predicate p is structural recursive, then no Prolog computation tree contains a recursive loop for p.

PROOF: By contradiction. We first observe that the well-founded ordering $>_t$ on ground terms can be directly extended to a well-founded ordering $>_{t'}$ on tuples of terms such that:

$$<t_1,...,t_n> \; >_{t'} \; <t_1',...,t_n'> \quad \Leftrightarrow \quad \forall i \in \{1,...,n\}: t_i \geq_t t_i' \; \wedge \; \exists j \in \{1,...,n\}: t_j >_t t_j'.$$

Now assume that for the Prolog computation rule there is a computed proof tree T for some queried program (P,G) with a recursive loop $L_0,...,L_i,...$ for p such that for all $j \geq i$ L_j is a p-literal. For each pair $L_j = p(t_1,...,t_n)$ and $L_{j+1} = p(t_1',...,t_n')$ there is a clause C_i for p such that L_j is an instance of the head of p and L_{j+1} is an instance of a recursive literal in C_j. Let $I = \{i_1,...,i_k\}$ be the subset of indices mentioned in 4.4.1. For all $i \in \{i_1,...,i_k\}$ t_i and t_i' are ground since P is well-moded and T is computed according to the Prolog computation rule. Thus we have

$$<t_{i1},...,t_{ik}> \; >_{t'} \; <t_{i1}',...,t_{ik}'>$$

contradicting the assumption that L_i, L_{i+1}, ... is an infinite sequence. ∎

4.4.3 EXAMPLE: *Structural Recursion: Merge*

Consider the following example taken from [NAI86]:

m_1: merge(X,[],X) .
m_2: merge([],X,X).
m_3: merge([A|X],[B|Y],[A|Z]) ← A ≤ B, merge(X,[B|Y],Z).
m_4: merge([A|X],[B|Y],[B|Z]) ← A > B, merge([A|X],Y,Z).

The intent is that merge(X,Y,Z) is true if Z is the merge of two sorted lists X and Y. We have mode(merge(+,+,-)). Starting to prove that merge terminates when called in this mode one soon realizes that there is no single argument which is decreasing at each recursive call. If the head of the first list is less than or equal to the head of the second list, the first argument of merge decreases, but in the other case the second argument decreases. However, at each recursive call at least one decreases while none increases. Thus merge is structural recursive, and theorem 4.4.2 guarantees termination. ■

The well-founded ordering mentioned in def. 4.4.1 can be any one of the well-founded orderings mentioned in section 3.4. A special and most common example is the subterm ordering. Taking this order and restricting the set of indices to a singleton we get something what is analogous to primitive recursive functions (see [BOE85]).

4.4.4 DEFINITION: *Primitive recursive procedures*

The procedure definition of a structural recursive procedure π for a predicate p is called primitive recursive if (using the notations of 4.4.1)

- The well-founded ordering '$>_g$' is the subterm ordering.
- The set of indices I is a singleton.
- There is at most one recursive literal in each clause.
- All predicates on which p depends are primitive recursive. ■

4.4.5 PROPOSITION: *Primitive Recursion terminates*

A query ← p(t$_1$,...,t$_n$) terminates if p is primitive recursive.

PROOF: If p is primitive recursive, then all predicates q on which p depends, are primitive recursive as well. Theorem 4.4.2 implies that none of these predicates has a recursive loop. This implies termination. ■

A well-known example for primitive recursion is the 'append' procedure, with I = {1}.

From the point of view of syntax, this concept of primitive recursion in logic programming is slightly more general than its original meaning since in logic programming

- relations are defined, not functions;
- terms are reduced to subterms, not natural numbers to their predecessors.

Note that above we have given a *syntactical* characterization of a primitive recursive procedure *definition*. The question is undecidable in general whether for a given function there exists a primitive recursive definition. Obviously the same is true for the question whether a relation, specified in a logic programming language, has a primitive recursive definition.

Actually, most real programs specify primitive recursive relations or functions. Thus the expressive power of primitive recursion seems to be sufficient for most real problems. Each function which can be calculated on a Turing machine in a number of steps which has an primitive recursive upper bound is in fact primitive recursive, as is shown in [SCH74].

The view that primitive recursive data types capture the majority of data types that arise in programming practice has been expressed by Cremers and Hibbard [CRH80]. They have proposed an expression-oriented primitive recursive specification language based on a scheme similar to what has been called structural recursion above.

The procedure (or function) definitions, as written down by the programmer, however, are not primitive recursive quite often.

4.4.6 EXAMPLE: *Primitive Recursion for 'perm'*

Consider, for instance, the perm example given above. We repeat it here.

p_1:   perm([],[]).
p_2:   perm(L,[H|T])   ←   append^2(V,[H|U],L),
                                         append^1(V,U,W),
                                         perm(W,T).

There is no subterm relation between the input arguments 'L' and 'W' in the second clause, so this *definition* is not primitive recursive. The relation perm, however, is of course primitive recursive, as the following equivalent definition shows:

p_1':   perm([],[]).
p_2':   perm([X|L],Z)   ←   perm(L,Y), insert(X,Y,Z).
i_1:   insert(X,[],[X]).
i_2:   insert(X,L,[X|L]).
i_3:   insert(X,[H|L1],[H|L2])   ←   insert(X,L1,L2).

The declarative meaning of both definitions is the same: perm(L1,L2) holds if the list L2 is a permutation of the list L1. Procedurally, there is a difference in the way how permutations of a given list are generated: while in the first definition an arbitrary element of a given list becomes the first element of the result, in the second definition the first element is removed and then inserted in an arbitrary position. In the second definition *insert* is primitive recursive since, for the second argument, 'L1' is a proper subterm of '[H|L1]', and *perm* is primitive recursive since *insert* is and 'L' is a proper subterm of '[H|L]'.

Identification of primitive recursion is a rather straightforward method to prove termination for well-moded programs: it needs only *syntactical* means. The identification of safe modes which guarantee data driven computation involves dataflow analysis. Efficient techniques for this task are well-known (see [DEB88] for details). An outline of such an approach to prove termination is given in Ricci's diploma thesis (see [RIC87]). It has also identified the problem of local variables and proposed to approach this problem by integration of partial evaluation techniques.

An approach to identify primitive recursion by *program transformation* has been described by Aquilano, Barbuti, Bocchetti and Martelli (see [ABB86] and [BAM87]). It involves dataflow analysis which the authors call 'identification of admissible I/0-selections'. The idea is to check if a Horn clause procedure can be transformed to primitive recursive functions such that the relation it defines can be regarded as the set-theoretic union of primitive recursive functions. There remain, however, severe restrictions. We mention only some of them. The program must be deterministic, i.e., no two clause heads are unifiable. Recursion must be linear, i.e., each procedure may have at most one recursive clause, and each recursive clause may have only one recursive literal. Mutual recursion is disallowed.

Barbuti and Martelli have studied the problem of termination in the context of deductive databases and negation in order to characterize ground atomic formulas which can be regarded as *categorical* (see 2.4). They advocate to follow a 'functional style of programming' in order to achieve termination results automatically. In this vein Ficarelli has taken the approach to transform logic programs - if possible - to term rewriting systems and then to apply one of the techniques developed in that area, namely recursive path ordering, to prove termination [FIC88].

A different way to tackle the problem of dataflow has been proposed by Lee Naish in the context of MU-Prolog [NAI86]. In MU-Prolog programs are augmented by wait-declarations which specify the conditions under which goals can be evaluated. The effect of such wait-declarations is that the evaluation of a goal is delayed until some arguments are sufficiently generated, i.e., bound to non-variable terms. Naish gives an algorithm which generates wait-declarations for recursive procedures. The idea is to detect sets of arguments where one is guaranteed to decrease and none in the set increase in any recursive call if these arguments are sufficiently bound. Our definition of structural recursion given above is based on this idea.

Wait declarations cause dynamic reordering of subgoals and thus allow coroutined execution of Prolog programs. In so far they give a powerful technique to control program execution by some specification of the flow of data. Mode declarations specify dataflow in a static way. With regard to termination they serve the same purpose. They ensure that certain arguments are properly bound when a recursive goal is evaluated.

4.5 Bounded Recursion

Primitive and structural recursion, as discussed in the last section, can be regarded as special cases of a more general situation, which can informally be described by the property that recursion reduces problems to *strictly* smaller ones. Simplicity of structural and primitive recursion stems from the fact that this decrease of problem size can be recognized by syntactical means. A more general situation can be characterized by the property, that arguments occurring in a - succeeding or failing - derivation must not exceed a certain length which is a function of the length of the greatest input argument. The following notion is similar to what has been introduced by van Gelder [GEL87].

4.5.1 DEFINITION: *Bounded Term Size Property*

A well moded program P has the bounded term size property if there exists a function $f(n)$ such that, for any SLD derivation $G = G_0, G_1,...,G_k$, whenever G is well moded and has no argument t_i with $|t_i| > n$, then no subgoal in G_i $(0 < i \le k)$ has an argument whose term size exceeds $f(n)$, whether the derivation is successful or not. We also say that for such a program recursion is bounded. ∎

The important difference between van Gelders definition and ours is that we additionally claim that the queried program is well moded. If data driven program evaluation is not guaranteed, such a definition would not make much sense in our context. Even the append-procedure would not have the bounded term size property, as the the top-level goal ←append(X,Y,Z) illustrates. Thus it is necessary to impose a further restriction on the program and the entry goal.

Besides, as pointed out in [GEL87] it is undecidable in general whether a given program has the bounded term size property.

Note that bounded recursion does not imply that a standard interpreter terminates.

The following example illustrates some interesting aspects of bounded recursion.

4.5.2 EXAMPLE: *Algebraic Simplification of Arithmetic Terms*

/*ADDITION*/

s_{01}: s(A+(B+C),D)	←s((A+B)+C,D).	/*Associativity*/
s_{02}: s(A+B,C)	←s(B+A,C).	/*Commutativity*/
s_{03}: s(X+0,0).		/*Zero*/
s_{04}: s(X+Y,Z)	←s(X,A), s(Y,B), s(A+B,Z).	/*Simplify Subterms*/
s_{05}: s(A+B,C)	←number(A), number(B), C is A+B.	/*Evaluate if possible*/

/*MULTIPLICATION */

s_{06}: s(A*(B*C),D)	←s((A*B)*C,D).	/*Associativity*/
s_{07}: s(A*B,C)	←s(B*A,C).	/*Commutativity*/
s_{08}: s(X*1,Y)	←s(X,Y).	/*One*/
s_{09}: s(X*0,0).		/*Zero*/
s_{10}: s(X*Y,Z)	←s(X,A), s(Y,B), s(A*B,Z).	/*Simplify Subterms*/
s_{11}: s(A*B,C)	←number(A), number(B), C is A*B.	/*Evaluate if possible*/
s_{12}: s(A,A).		/*Reflexivity*/

This program logically implies for instance that the term

$$3*4*a + 1*b,$$

can be simplified to $12 * a + b$. Therefore, for the query

$$\leftarrow s(3*4*a + 1*b, X)$$

we would like to get $X = 12*a + b$ as computed answer. The Prolog interpreter, however, will loop forever, interchanging the two summands of the term repeatedly. The cause of this loop is the program clause s_{02}, which expresses the commutativity of addition. This clause gives rise to the recursive branch

$$s(3*4*a + 1*b , X),$$
$$s(1*b + 3*4*a, X'),$$
$$s(3*4*a + 1*b , X''),$$
$$...$$

The same problem arises from clause s_{07}, which expresses commutativity of multiplication.

Program clauses s_{04} and s_{10} do not necessarily reduce the first argument to a smaller term in the third body literal because of the commutativity axioms and because of reflexivity.

Clause s_{12} can be regarded as reflexivity axiom, stating that every term can be reduced to itself. Normally one would like to state quite a different thing in the given context, namely that simplification should be done recursively as long (or as deep) as possible. This could easily be expressed in a term rewriting systems, but it is not so easy to express it in pure Prolog. The Prolog programmer often tends to use impure features as the cut, or he would use negation to express the fact that s_{12} should only be used if no other clause is applicable.

Clauses which are obviously reducing are s_{03}, s_{08} and s_{09}. Clauses s_{11} and s_{05} are reducing, if numbers have constant weight. However, if a linear term norm is used, there is no way to show that the rules of associativity for addition and multiplication (s_{01} and s_{06}) cannot cause recursive loops. Such a proof, however, could be done with RPO using a right-to-left status for '+' and '*' (see 3.4.3). RPO also allows to derive that the following clause s_{13}, expressing the law of distributivity, does not cause loops if its first argument is bound:

$$s_{13}: s(A*(B+C),D) \quad \leftarrow s(A*B+A*C),D)$$

Despite the problems the Prolog interpreter has with this quite familiar example, the problem itself is not very difficult. None of the clauses given above enlarge the terms constructed at recursive calls, and thus the procedure 's' given above has the property of bounded recursion. The question arises which mechanism would be appropriate to cope with this sort of problems.

Several authors have studied the problem of how to avoid undesired and unnecessary loops by modification of the Prolog interpreter. A general approach is to identify those expansions of a proof tree which lead to redundant subgoals. A goal G in a proof tree T is redundant with regard to an ancestor goal G' if expansion of G does not lead to a so-lution of G which cannot be derived by another expansion of the G-rooted subtree of T.

The problem is how to detect redundancy. A first idea, as proposed for instance in [COV85], is simple loop checking. It assumes that some goal G is redundant with an ancestor goal G' if G and G' are unifiable. Loop checking then discards those matching subgoals, i.e., they are assumed to fail.

As pointed out by Poole and Goebel in [POG85], such an approach destroys completeness. This fact is illustrated by the following example.

4.5.3 EXAMPLE: *Simple Loop Checking is Incomplete*

1) *Subgoal is more general than ancestor goal*
   p(b).
   p(a) ← p(X).
   ← p(a).

2) *Subgoal is less general than ancestor goal*
   p(a).
   q(b).
   p(X) ← p(a).
   ← p(X), q(X).

3) *Subgoal and ancestor goal refer to independent variables*
   p(a).
   q(b).
   p(X) ← p(Y).
   ← p(X), q(X).

In all these examples, the clauses can be reordered to generate infinite branches. If subgoals are discarded whenever they *match* an ancestor goal, correct derivations would not be found in all these cases. In [ABK89] Apt et al. have recently shown that no simple sound and complete loop check exists even for programs without functions symbols.

The following theorem, however, identifies special cases where simple loop checking is safe.

4.5.4 THEOREM: *Restricted Loop Checking is Safe.*

Suppose that in a proof tree G is an ancestor goal of G'. If G and G' are unifiable and the variables occurring in G and G' are bound to the same variables, then G' is redundant.

PROOF: See [POG85]

The assumption of theorem 4.5.4 is satisfied for example 4.5.2. at all critical places. Take clause s_{02} as an example. In a data driven evaluation the first argument of 's' will always be ground. The only variable occurrences then are at the second argument, and those variables are identical. Thus for example 4.5.2 simple loop checking is safe.

There is another sufficient condition for the safety of simple loop checking which is due to Smith, Genesereth and Ginsberg:

4.5.5 THEOREM: *Loop Checking for Single Answer Queries*

If T is a proof tree for a single literal query G and only one answer for G is needed, any subgoal G' that is an instance of G can be discarded. Repeated ground queries and repeated functional queries, where only one answer, if any, exists, can always be discarded. ■

PROOF: see [SGG87].

In [SGG87] it is further argued that the depth of repetition of matching subgoals which has to be allowed to ensure completeness depends on the number of answers for the given goal. To state in advance how many answers are needed, is difficult, if not impossible. There is, however, an algorithm, independently discovered by several authors ([BLA68], [MKS81],[TAS86], [SGG87]) that tackles this problem by a modified inter-

preter. These modifications go beyond simple loop checking. To describe this algorithm, we need some further notions taken from [SEI88].

OLD resolution is the special case of SLD resolution where always the leftmost atom is
selected. For a node v in an OLD-tree len(v) denotes the number of its atoms.

4.5.6 Definition: *Unit Subrefutation*

Consider a path from a node v_1 in an OLD tree to one of its descendants v_2 such that for
every node v on the path other than v_2 len(v) > len(v_2) holds. Let v be $\leftarrow A_1,...,A_n$,
where n = len(v_1) and let k = n - len(v_2). The path from v_1 to v_2 can be regarded as a
refutation of $\leftarrow A_1,...,A_k$ by neglecting the last len(v_2) atoms in every goal on that
path. This path is called *subrefutation* of $\leftarrow A_1,...,A_k$. If k = 1, it is called *unit
subrefutation*.

4.5.7 DEFINITION: *OLDT Structure*

An *OLDT structure* is a partial OLDT tree Tr with two tables, a *solution table* Ts and a
lookup table Tl. Every node of the OLDT-tree is classified as either a *solution node* or
as a *lookup node*. A solution table is a set of entries. Each entry consists of a pair of a
key and a list (called a solution list) where the key is a positive atom and the solution list
is a list of atoms such that each atom in the list is an instance of its key. A lookup table
Tl of (Tr,Ts) is a set of pointers pointing from each lookup node in Tr into a solution
list of some key K in Ts such that the leftmost atom of the lookup node is an instance of
K. The tail list of a solution list pointed from a lookup node is called the *associated
solution list* of the lookup node.

4.5.8 DEFINITION: *Initial OLDT Structure*

Given a queried program $\Pi = (P,G)$, the initial OLDT structure is the triple
$T_0 = (Tr_0,Ts_0,Tl_0)$ where Tr_0 is the single node v_0 labeled with G, Ts_0 is the solution
table consisting of only one entry whose key is the leftmost atom of G with an empty
solution list, and Tl_0 is empty. The node v_0 is classified as a solution node.

4.5.9 DEFINITION: *Extension of an OLDT Structure*

Given a queried program $\Pi = (P,G)$ and an OLDT structure $T = (Tr,Ts,Tl)$ for Π. An immediate extension of T by P is the result of applying (if possible) one of the following operations:

(1) Select a node v in Tr, labeled with $\leftarrow A, \Gamma$, where A is an atom and Γ is a (possible empty) sequence of atoms.

- *(OLD extension)* If v is a terminal solution node, let $C_1,...,C_k$ be all the clauses (if any) in P such that each C_i is of the form $B_i \leftarrow \Delta_i$ and A and B_i have the mgu θ_i. Then add k child nodes labeled with each $G_1,...,G_k$ to v, where each G_i is $\leftarrow (\Delta_i,\Gamma)\theta_i$. The edge from v to node G_i is labeled with θ_i. When there exists no such clause, v is called a failure leaf.

- *(lookup extension)* If v is a lookup node and its associated solution list is not empty, let $B_1\tau_1,...,B_k\tau_k$ be all the elements in that list such that A and $B_i\tau_i$ have the mgu θ_i, and let G_i be $\Gamma\theta_i$. Then add k child nodes $G_1,...,G_k$ to v. The edge from v to node G_i is labelled with θ_i.

(2) If the above lookup extension is performed to a node v, then replace the pointer from v by one pointing to the end of its associated solution list.

(3) After the above operations, if a new node labeled with a null clause is derived, then it is called a success leaf. A new node labeled with a non-null clause is classified as a lookup node if the leftmost atom of the new node is an instance of some key in Ts. Otherwise it is a solution node.

(4) For a new lookup node (if any), add a pointer from it to the head of the solution list of the corresponding key.

(5) For a new solution node (if any) add a new entry whose key is the leftmost atom of the label of the new node and whose solution list is the empty list. If a new node is a lookup node, add no entry. For each unit subrefutation of atom L (if any) starting from a solution node and ending with a new node, add its solution $L\lambda$ to the end of the solution list of L in Ts, if $L\lambda$ is not in the solution list.

4.5.10 DEFINITION: *OLDT-refutation*

For a queried program $\Pi = (P,G)$ an OLDT refutation is a path in some extension of the initial OLDT structure for Π from the root to a node labeled with the empty clause. ∎

Note that an OLDT refutation from $\Pi = (P,G)$ is an SLD refutation from (P',G) where P' is P plus some unit clause theorems of P. Thus soundness of OLDT is implied by the soundness of SLD. A completeness proof of OLDT has been given by Tamaki and Sato in [TAS85]. They have further shown that OLDT always terminates and gives a finite set of solutions for programs with finite Herbrand models.

A further completeness result for programs with the bounded term size property has been given by Seki and Itoh in [SEI88]. The following theorem is a slight modification of what they have established.

4.5.11 THEOREM: *OLDT and the Bounded Term Size Property*

Assume that a (definite) program P has the bounded term size property. Then for any single literal goal G the search for an OLDT-refutation is finite, whether the search is successful or not. ■

PROOF: The proof is along the lines of [SEI88]. The bounded term size property for P implies that the length of a solution list is bounded from above by a constant. Hence the branching factor of each lookup node is bounded by a constant. The length of a path is also bounded by a constant since the number of solution nodes is bounded by a constant and every lookup node in a path reduces the number of atoms in the label by one. Thus the size of an OLDT structure is bounded by a constant. ■

The bounded term size property of programs is undecidable in general. The search for sufficient conditions has been identified as a "research area in its own right" by Seki / Itoh and by van Gelder ([SEI88], [GEL87]). We will give an answer to this problem in chapter 7.

Chapter 5

THE PROBLEM OF LOCAL VARIABLES

In this chapter we discuss the problems local variables cause in termination proofs. We show that all Turing computable functions can be specified by (definite) logic programs without local variables. From a pragmatic point of view local variables are important, however, and there seems to be no chance to facilitate termination proofs by means of removing local variables via program transformation.

5.1 Local Variables and Term Orderings

Recursion, if terminating, reduces problems to smaller ones. The context of logic programming suggests measuring problem sizes by term norms. It is a rather easy task to prove termination for structural or primitive recursion. In those cases the reduction of problem size can be recognized by syntactical means. If the terms to be compared have different sets of variable occurrences, techniques based on syntactical analysis are not sufficient. The following easy example illustrates this problem:

We have

$$|f(g(X))|_n > |g(X)|_n, \qquad \text{and also}$$
$$|f(g(X))\sigma|_n > |g(X)\sigma|_n \qquad \text{for all instantiations } \sigma,$$

since the right term is in all cases a proper subterm of the left one.

On the other hand, although

$|f(g(X))|_n > |g(Y)|_n$ is valid,

$|f(g(X))\theta|_n > |g(Y)\theta|_n$ is not valid for arbitrary instantiations θ.

The problem is that the right term has a variable not occurring in the left one. Although $g(Y)$ is matching a subterm of $f(g(X))$, it is not identical with a subterm of that term. As to the substitution $\theta = \{X/c, Y/g(g(c))\}$ we get that $g(Y)\theta$ is actually greater than $f(g(X))\theta$. Thus the partial ordering induced by the n-norm is not stable under substitution. Stability under substitution is quite difficult, if possible, to achieve if different variable sets are allowed in the terms to be compared. The subterm relation, for instance, needs that the smaller term has no variables not occurring in the greater one.

5.1.1 DEFINITION: *Local variables in recursive clauses*

A recursive clause $C_i \in \pi = \{C_1,\ldots,C_n\}$ in a moded program is said to have local variables if there is a variable v and a recursive literal c_{ij} such that $v \in \text{in}(c_{ij}) \wedge v \notin \text{in}(c_{i0})$, where c_{i0} is the head of C_i. A procedure is said to have local variables if it has a recursive clause with local variables. ∎

In the context of data driven program evaluation (see 3.2) such a local variable is guaranteed to be ground when the recursive literal is called. Therefore a value must have been computed for that variable before. If the program is well moded, then there is some literal on the left with v on an output position. Generally, if variables which do not occur at the corresponding clause's head, occur at a recursive literal's input positions, then there must be other body literals which relate the input variables of both literals.

5.1.2 EXAMPLE: *Quicksort*

q_1:   qsort([],[]).

q_2:   qsort([H|L],S)   ←   split(H,L,[],[],A,B),
                                               qsort(A,A_1), qsort(B,B_1),
                                               append(A_1,[H|B_1],S).

s_1:   split(H,[X|L],A,B,A_1,B_1)   ←   X≤H, split(H,L,[X|A],B,A_1,B_1).

s_2:   split(H,[X|L],A,B,A_1,B_1)   ←   X>H, split(H,L,A,[X|B],A_1,B_1).

s_3:   split(H,[],A,B,A,B).

The procedure qsort, which has mode(qsort(+,-)), implements Hoare's well known quicksort algorithm: the tail L of the input list [H|L] is split into two sublists A and B, such that all elements of A are less than or equal to H, and all elements of B are greater than H. This work is done by split, which has mode(split(+,+,+,+,-,-)). When split is called, its third and fourth argument are bound to the empty list.* The sublists A and B are then recursively sorted by qsort, and the resulting lists A_1 and B_1 are then concatenated by append, putting the element 'H' between. The values of A and B, which are input of the recursive calls of qsort, and [H|L], the input of the head of q_2, are related by split(H,L,[],[],A,B).

This situation, where a comparison of the sizes of [H|L] and A or B is needed, suggests looking for an inequality for split and deriving an inequalitiy relating the relevant terms. Such an approach goes beyond syntactical analysis, since an inequality for split refers to the meaning of that predicate.

In order to check whether or not the two inequalities

LI_1: |[H|L]θ| > |Aθ| and
LI_2: |[H|L]θ| > |Bθ|

are valid, instead of considering all instantiations θ one only has to consider those ground substitutions θ which are correct answers to the goal split(L,H,A,B). While the two inequalities above can be proved for this restricted set of substitutions, this proof could not be achieved for an arbitrary instantiation. LI_1 and LI_2 would not be valid if we take θ = {H/1,L/[],A/[1,2],B/[1,2]} for instance. That substitution, however, is not a correct answer to split(L,H,A,B) and thus needs not to be taken into account.

5.2 Turing Computability

With regard to Turing computability, local variables are not necessary in a logic program: every function, which can be computed by a Turing machine, can be computed by

---

* The procedure split could be specified in a simpler way. We use this tail-recursive version of split for the sake of an argument which is discussed later. It facilitates transformation into a form without local variables.

a well moded Horn clause program without mutual recursion which has no local variables.

5.2.1 DEFINITION: *Turing Computable Functions*

We say that a function f(x) is Turing computable, if its value can be computed by some Turing machine (TM for short) T_f, which initially has a tape holding exactly the argument x. When T_f stops, its tape contains the value of the function f(x). ∎

Thus for each Turing computable function f there is some special Turing machine T_f. A well known result of computability theory is that there exists one machine, the universal Turing machine, that can compute all Turing computable functions (see [MIN67]). This universal Turing machine imitates the computation of each Turing machine T_f, given a description of the Turing machine T_f and an argument x of T_f.

Here we do something similar. We give a Horn clause program which takes as input the program of a Turing machine T_f and an argument x of T_f.

5.2.2 EXAMPLE: *Universal Turing Machine (With Local Variables)*

m_1: member(H,[H|L]).

m_2: member(X,[H|L])   ← member(X,L).

t_1:   turing(t(X,Y,Z),S,P,t(X,Y,Z))   ← member(p(S,Y,**halt**,W,D),P).

t_2:   turing(t(X,Y,[R|L]),S,P,T)   ← member(p(S,Y,S',W,r),P),
                                            turing(t([W|X],R,L),S',P,T).

t_3:   turing(t(X,Y,[]),S,P,T)   ← member(p(S,Y,S',W,r),P),
                                            turing(t([W|X],' ',[]),S',P,T).

t_4:   turing(t([X|L],Y,R),S,P,T)   ← member(p(S,Y,S',W,l),P),
                                            turing(t(L,X,[W|R]),S',P,T).

t_5:   turing(t([],Y,R),S,P,T)   ← member(p(S,Y,S',W,l),P),
                                            turing(t([],' ',[W|R]),S',P,T).

The tape of the Turing machine T_f is represented by a term of the form t([L|LEFT],X,[R|RIGHT]), if it is nonempty in both directions. The lists [L|LEFT] and [R|RIGHT] denote parts of the machine's tape on the left and on the right of the head of T_f respectively. The square under the head of T_f has the content X. The variable L denotes the square on the left of X, R denotes the square on the right of X. This situation is illustrated by the figure given below.

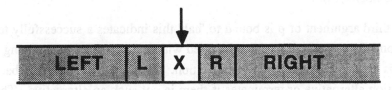

By ' ' we denote the blank symbol. The empty list [] denotes a part of the tape consisting of blanks only.

Variables S and S' represent the current state of the machine.
The variable P specifies the program of T_f. When the procedure turing is called, P is bound to a list of tuples

p(State,Symbol,New_State,Write,Direction) where

State	represents the current State.
New_state	represents the successor state. When bound to **halt** the computation successfully terminates.
Symbol	is bound to the symbol currently under the head of the machine.
Write	is bound to the Symbol which will be written.
Direction	is either l or r indicating that the head is next moving left or right.

The goal, which invokes the Turing machine's computation, has the form

turing(tape(X,Y,Z),S,P,T)

where tape(X,Y,Z), S and P specify respectively the initial tape description, the initial state and the program for T_f. In the final state, if ever, T is bound to the content of the tape.

The procedure member identifies the command of the TM program to be executed next. In the context of program 5.2.2 it is called with its second argument bound to a list P, representing the program of T_f. This list is ground. The first argument of member is bound to a term with functor p. The first two arguments of this term, representing the current state and the symbol currently under the head, are ground, while the other three arguments are variables. Thus the first argument has to be regarded as output, while the second one is input. Thus we get

  mode(member(-,+)).

When the third argument of p is bound to 'halt' this indicates a successfully terminating computation. By contrast, if member is called with its second argument being the empty list, there is an unsuccessful partial computation. Then the machine either backtracks to a computation alternative or terminates if there is not such an alternative. This computational behaviour is due to the nondeterminism of member and gives a nondeterministic machine.

For the procedure turing we have

  mode(turing(+,+,+,-))

indicating that the last argument is output. This argument will be bound to the content of the tape after a successful computation, if ever.

Thus the program of example 5.2.2 specifies a universal Turing machine. Its operational semantics simulates the operations of that machine. Obviously this program is free of mutual recursion, and it can easily be recognized that it is well moded. Considering the clauses t_2 - t_5, however, one sees that the variables S' and W are local. We can, however, transform that program into one without local variables. This program is given in example 5.2.3.

5.2.3 EXAMPLE: *Universal Turing Machine (Without Local Variables)*

t_1: exec(t(X,Y,Z),   S,[p(S,Y,**halt**,W,D)|P'],P,t(X,Y,Z)).

t_2: exec(t(X,Y,[R|L]), S,[p(S,Y,S',W,**r**)|P'],P,T) ← exec(t([W|X],R,L),S',P,P,T).

t_3: exec(t(X,Y,[]),   S,[p(S,Y,S',W,**r**)|P'],P,T) ← exec(t([W|X],' ',[]),S',P,P,T).

t_4: exec(t([X|L],Y,R), S,[p(S,Y,S',W,**l**)|P'],P,T) ← exec(t(L,X,[W|R]),S',P,P,T).

t_5: exec(t([],Y,R),   S,[p(S,Y,S',W,**l**)|P'],P,T) ← exec(t([],' ',[W|R]),S',P,P,T).

t_6: exec(T,   S,[H|P'],P,T')   ← exec(T,S,P',P,T').

The idea is to define one procedure exec which gets the tasks of both turing and member. We need an additional argument, which is the third one in exec, where the TM program is scanned. The clauses t_1 - t_5 assume that the first element of that list (which is actually a sublist of the originally given program, saved in the fourth argument) is a TM command which applies to the current state S and the currently read symbol Y. If this is true, the TM command is executed and exec is recursively called in its new state with a modified tape, now having the complete program P as its third argument.

If, however, the head of the list in the third argument represents a TM command which is not applicable to the current situation, then only t_6 is applicable, which is the counterpart of the clause m_2 in the former program. Thus the operations of the program in 5.2.2 are simulated by the one in 5.2.3.

5.2.4 THEOREM: *Turing Computability*

For each Turing computable function f there is a well moded Horn clause program P_f without mutual recursion and local variables such that P_f computes f.

PROOF: The proof is by the program given in 5.2.3. ∎

This construction has been adapted from one given in [TAR75], which, however, is mutual recursive. A result which is similar to theorem 5.2.4 has been achieved in [RIC88]. Other examples using the same proof idea can be found in [BOE87].

5.3 Local Variables and Computed Values

In order to handle the problem of local variables one could think of removing them by program transformation, generalizing the technique used to transform program 5.2.2 in program 5.2.3. It is quite unlikely, however, that such an approach would facilitate automatic termination proofs.

We take the quicksort algorithm as an example. The following is a transformed version of the procedure given in 5.1.2.

5.3.1 EXAMPLE: *Quicksort without Local Variables*

q_0:   qsort([],[]).

q_1:   qsort([H|L],S)   ← qsort$_1$([H|L],H,L,[],[],S).

q_2:   qsort$_1$([],_,_,[],[],[]).

q_3:   qsort$_1$([A],_,_,[],[],[A]).

q_4:   qsort$_1$([H|L],H,[X|Xs],A,B,S)   ← X≤H, qsort$_1$([H|L],H,Xs,[X|A],B,S).

q_5:   qsort$_1$([H|L],H,[X|Xs],A,B,S)   ← X>H, qsort$_1$([H|L],H,Xs,A,[X|B],S).

q_6:   qsort$_1$([H|L],H,[],[A$_1$|A],[B$_1$|B],S)   ← qsort$_1$([A$_1$|A],A$_1$,A,[],[],A$_2$),
                                                          qsort$_1$([B$_1$|B],B$_1$,B,[],[],B$_2$),
                                                          append(A$_2$,[H|B$_2$],S).

q_7:   qsort$_1$([H|L],H,[],[],[B$_1$|B],[H|B$_2$])   ← qsort$_1$([B$_1$|B],B$_1$,B,[],[],B$_2$).

q_8:   qsort$_1$([H|L],H,[],[A$_1$|A],[],S)   ← qsort$_1$([A$_1$|A],A$_1$,A,[],[],A$_2$),
                                                          append(A$_2$,[H],S). ■

Although this set of clauses is harder to comprehend than the original one given in 5.1.2, the operational behaviour of the latter is simulated by the new one. The task of sorting a nonempty list is given from qsort to the procedure qsort$_1$ with arity 6. The first argument of qsort$_1$ is bound to the list to be sorted. The second and third argument are bound to the head and the tail of the initially given input list. The further two arguments are needed for splitting the input list. The last argument will be bound to the sorted list.

Clauses q_2 and q_3 are handling the trivial cases of lists with zero or one element. Clauses q_4 and q_5 are doing the job of splitting a given list in two sublists. This job is finished as soon as the third argument is bound to the empty list. In this situation one of the clauses q_6, q_7 or q_8 becomes applicable. These three clauses are the counterpart of the second qsort clause in 5.1.2. One of the clauses q_6, q_7 or q_8 is used depending on whether one of the sublists resulting from splitting is empty.

With the following annotations

mode(qsort(+,-))
mode(qsort$_1$(+,+,+,+,+,-))

we realize that the program is well moded. If the first five arguments are taken as input, there is obviously no local variable either.

The task of proving termination, however, is now even harder than before. With regard to the whole set of input indices $\{1,...,5\}$ $qsort_1$ is not structurally recursive. Taking clause q_4 as an example one sees that whereas the third argument is decreased, the fourth one is increased to the same degree. Starting with this clause one realizes that only such index sets are reasonable which have 3 but not 4 as an element. Clause q_6, however, shows that the absence of 4 in the index set results in getting the local variables A and A_1.

So the problem caused by the local variables in the quicksort procedure as specified in 5.1.2 has essentially not been removed by that transformation. What happened is that the result of the task of splitting is removed from input argument position 4 (or 5) to the first input argument position by clause q_6.

The problem of local variables in Prolog is actually the problem of computed values given as arguments to recursive calls. The problem of computed values is thus the essence of the given problem. This problem has the shape of the local variable problem in Prolog since Prolog has no evaluation of expressions. The task of evaluating the expression, $3 + 4$, for instance, with the binary '+' as principal functor is specified in Prolog by the goal $\leftarrow$plus(3,4,X) with the ternary predicate symbol 'plus', having X as local variable. Local variables in well moded programs thus often represent the results of evaluating expressions.

Programs in functional programming languages often do not have that use of local variables which is characteristic of Prolog programs. We take pure Lisp as an example. Straightforward transliteration of the qsort program of example 5.1.2 in pure Lisp yields the program given in example 5.3.2.

Note that there is no local variable occurrence in this program. There is, however, a new problem. The recursive terms

(i)   `(qsort (car(split (car L) (cdr L))))`   and
(ii)   `(qsort (cdr(split (car L) (cdr L))))`

are actually greater than the original term `(qsort L)` for any simplification ordering (see 3.4.1). There is also the problem of non-linearity: the same input variable L occurs more than once as argument of recursive calls in the body of qsort.

5.3.2 EXAMPLE: *Qsort in Pure Lisp*

```
(define (split H L)
  (cond ((null? L)
         (cons nil nil))
        ((<= (car L) H)
         (cons (cons (car L)
                     (car (split H (cdr L))))
               (cdr (split H (cdr L)))))
        ((> (car L) H )
         (cons (car (split H ( cdr L)))
               (cons (car L)
                     (cdr (split H (cdr L))))))))


(define (qsort L)
  (cond ((null? L) nil)
        (else (append
                (qsort(car(split (car L) (cdr L))))
                (cons(car L)
                     (qsort(cdr(split(car L)(cdr L))))))))
```

Both problems mentioned arise from the need to use explicit selectors like 'car' and 'cdr'. They do not occur in this form if one considers a functional language like ML, which facilitates a more pattern oriented style of programming. Example 5.3.3 gives the quicksort algorithm in ML.

5.3.3 EXAMPLE: *Qsort in ML*

```
fun  split   (a : int) []   =        ([],[])
   | split   a        (b::x) =        let val (l,r) = split a x in
                                      if a < b  then (l,b::r)
                                                else (b::l,r)
                                      end;
```

```
fun qsort  []        =    []
  | qsort  (a::x)     =    let val (l,r) = split a x in
                           (qsort l) @ (a::qsort r)
                           end;
```

In this notation we have exactly the same problem as in Prolog: to prove termination of qsort one needs to show that both 'l' and 'r' are strictly smaller then 'a::x'. Here the local variables 'l' and 'r' resulting from the evaluation of 'split a x' play the same role as the local variables 'A' and 'B' in example 5.1.2.

All the different ways to write down the quicksort algorithm which have been considered above illustrate the fact that the one and the same problem occurs with different shapes in different languages, depending on the style of programming these languages suggest.

Having identified 'computed values' as the core of the problem of local variables in Prolog, the view is confirmed that this problem cannot be handled by mere syntactical techniques in a reasonably general way. Instead the approximative characterization of the relation between in- and out-arguments by inequalities of the form specified in 3.4.12 seems to be a promising approach. Such an approach will be given in the next chapters.

Chapter 6

AND/OR DATAFLOW GRAPHS

Our general aim is to handle local variables by linear predicate inequalities. One of the basic problems in this context is the derivation of size relations among variables occurring in *compound goals*. In this chapter we introduce the notion of *AND/OR data flow graphs* and give an approach to this problem.

If nothing else is explicitly stated, in this chapter the norm |...| will always denote the restriction of the n-norm to ground terms. We assume that the given program is normalized, well-moded, and has no mutual recursion.

6.1 Problem Statement

A simple instance of the problem of this chapter is given by the quicksort algorithm which was already mentioned in the last chapter. For the sake of brevity and simplicity we give here a slightly different notation.

6.1.1 Example: *Quicksort*

q_1: qsort([],[]).

q_2: qsort([H|L],S)   ←   split(L,H,A,B), qsort(A,A_1), qsort(B,B_1), append(A_1,[H|B_1],S).

s_1: split([],Y,[],[]).

s_2: split([X|Xs],Y,[X|Ls],Bs)   ←   X ≤ Y, split(Xs,Y,Ls,Bs).

s_3: split([X|Xs],Y,Ls,[X|Bs])   ←   X > Y, split(Xs,Y,Ls,Bs).

It is assumed that a valid linear inequality for split has already been derived:

LI_{split} : $split_1 \geq$ $split_3 + split_4$

This inequality immediately implies for each instantiation θ satisfying split(L,H,A,B)

$\quad\quad |L\theta| \quad\quad \geq \quad\quad |A\theta| \quad$ and therefore

$\quad\quad |[H|L\theta]| \quad > \quad\quad |A\theta|$

which is the inequality needed to prove that the first recursive call of qsort in the body of q_2 terminates. The case for the second qsort-literal is analogous.

Generally, for a single–literal goal proposition 3.4.16 shows how to derive an inequality relating in- and out-variables.

The problem is more complicated for a compound goal. We start with a simple instance of that case.

6.1.2 EXAMPLE: *Linear Inequality for a Simple Compound Goal*

$\quad$ *goal:* $\quad\quad\quad\quad\quad \leftarrow$ p(U,V), q(f(V),W), r(W,g(X)), s(X,Y).
$\quad$ *inequalities:* $\quad\quad p_1 \geq p_2, q_1 \geq q_2, r_1 \geq r_2, s_1 \geq s_2,$

We are interested in an inequality relating U and Y. Let θ be a satisfying instantiation for $p(U,V)$, $q(f(V),W)$, $r(W,g(X))$, $s(X,Y)$.

There is the following chain of reasoning:

$\quad\quad |U\theta| \quad\quad \geq \quad |V\theta| \quad\quad$ by $p_1 \geq p_2$,
$\quad\quad |V\theta| + 1 \quad \geq \quad |W\theta| \quad\quad$ by $q_1 \geq q_2$ and proposition 3.4.16
$\quad\quad |W\theta| - 1 \quad \geq \quad |X\theta| \quad\quad$ by $r_1 \geq r_2$ and proposition 3.4.16
$\quad\quad |X\theta| \quad\quad \geq \quad |Y\theta| \quad\quad$ by $s_1 \geq s_2$, and therefore
$\quad\quad |U\theta| \quad\quad \geq \quad |Y\theta|.$

The simplicity of this example stems from the fact that the compound goal can directly be mapped into a chain of inequalities. This is possible since the dataflow in that example is actually linear: the output of one literal is the input of the next one.

The situation is more complicated in the next example.

6.1.3 EXAMPLE: *Confluent Dataflow in Qsort*

Consider the following compound goal

$\leftarrow$ split(L,H,A,B), qsort(A,A_1), qsort(B,B_1), append($A_1,[H|B_1],S$)

which is the body of the second qsort-clause in example 6.1.1. Let θ be an instantiation satisfying that goal. We are interested in an inequality relating L, H and S. The following inequalities are given:

LI_{split} :	$split_1$	$\geq$	$split_3 + split_4$
LI_{append} :	$append_1 + append_2$	$\geq$	$append_3$
LI_{qsort} :	$qsort_1$	$\geq$	$qsort_2$

The desired inequality can be derived as follows:

$|L\theta|$	$\geq$	$|A\theta| + |B\theta|$	by LI_{split}
$|A\theta|$	$\geq$	$|A_1\theta|$	by LI_{qsort}
$|B\theta|$	$\geq$	$|B_1\theta|$	by LI_{qsort}
$|A_1\theta| + |H\theta| + |B_1\theta| + 2$	$\geq$	$|S\theta|$	by LI_{append} and prop. 3.4.16

which gives $|L\theta| + |H\theta| + 2 \geq |S\theta|$.

There are several aspects in the last example worth to be mentioned. First of all, to give an upper bound on $S\theta$, we need to know about three different variables occurring on in-positions of append, namely A_1, B_1 and H.

H is in the set of variables which are compared, so the size of $H\theta$ can be assumed to be given. However, if the task had been to compare only L and S without taking H into account, there would be no solution. H occurs on no right side of an inequality, so there is no way to give an upper bound for its size.

A_1 and B_1 derive from processing the in-variables L and H. For the size of $A_1\theta$ there is an upper bound by $A\theta$, for the size of $B_1\theta$ there is an upper bound by $B\theta$. Both of A and B are related to L by the literal split(L,H,A,B). Fortunately, the sum of their sizes is bounded by the size of L, as LI_{split} implies. This situation is illustrated by figure 6.1.4 which shows that the flow of data in the body of qsort is *'confluent'*. This sort of confluence seems to be typical for *'divide and conquer'*-algorithms. Handling it in an appropriate way is crucial for the derivation of the desired inequality.

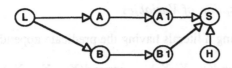

6.1.4 FIGURE: *Dataflow in the body of qsort₂*

In view of automatic termination proofs it is quite fortunate that the way of writing down the quicksort algorithm which logic programming suggests exhibits this confluent dataflow. As was illustrated above, ML is similar to Prolog in this respect. In contrast, the way one would specify quicksort in pure Lisp, would obscure confluence. As example 5.3.2 suggests, a function corresponding to split would have a compound result, containing two lists, and both recursive calls of qsort would acquire their input using explicit selector functions like car and cdr. We repeat the definition of qsort here:

```
(define(qsort L)
 (cond((null? L) nil)
    (else (append
              (qsort(car(split (car L) (cdr L))))
              (cons(car L)
                  (qsort(cdr(split(car L)(cdr L)))))))))
```

The use of explicit selectors results in the fact that the same variable L occurs twice in both recursive calls:

```
(qsort(car (split (car L) (cdr L))))
(qsort(cdr (split (car L) (cdr L))))
```

Apparently the variable L is *consumed* twice. The fact that different parts of the list structure which is bound to L are actually consumed can only be recognized with some knowledge about what is done by car and cdr. This is not visible on the syntactical surface.

When a variable is consumed more than once it is generally not possible to derive a valid linear inequality in the sense of def. 3.4.12.

6.1.5 EXAMPLE: *Multiple Consumption of Variables*

Consider the following goal containing n literals having the predicate append:

$$\text{append}(X_0,X_0,X_1), \text{append}(X_1,X_1,X_2),\ldots, \text{append}(X_{n-1},X_{n-1},X_n)$$

Because of the multiple variable occurrences this goal cannot be associated with a chain of linear inequalities fitting together such that X_0 and X_n can be related by one linear inequality. We have for some appropriate θ that

$$|X_0\theta| + |X_0\theta| \qquad\qquad \geq |X_1\theta| \qquad \text{and}$$
$$|X_1\theta| + |X_1\theta| \qquad\qquad \geq |X_2\theta| \qquad \text{which implies}$$
$$|X_0\theta| + |X_0\theta| + |X_0\theta| + |X_0\theta| \geq |X_2\theta|$$

Actually, if X_0 is bound to a list with k elements, X_n is bound to a list with $2^n {*} k$ elements. That the out-variable of the i-th literal is consumed twice by its successor gives rise to this factor which is exponential in the number of literals.

While multiple *consumption* of variables normally prevents the derivation of linear inequalities, multiple *generation* of variables causes *nondeterminism* in the derivation of inequalities, as the following example shows.

6.1.6 EXAMPLE: *Multiple Generation of Variables*

goal: $b(X,U), c(U,Y), d(X,V), e(V,Y).$
inequalities: $b_1 + 1 \geq b_2$
               $c_1 + 1 \geq c_2$
               $d_1 + 2 \geq d_2$
               $e_1 + 1 \geq e_2$

Suppose we want to infer an inequality relating X and Y.

X is related to Y by the two literals $b(X,U)$ and $c(U,Y)$, and this yields the inequality

$|X\theta_1| + 2 \geq |Y\theta_1|$ for an instantiation θ_1 satisfying $b(X,U),c(U,Y)$.

Another relation between X and Y is given by the two literals $d(X,V)$ and $e(V,Y)$, which implies

$|X\theta_2| + 3 \geq |Y\theta_2|$ for an instantiation θ_2 satisfying $d(X,V),e(V,Y)$.

Since there is a logical *'and'* connecting b(X,U), c(U,Y) and d(X,V), e(V,Y), both inequalities hold.

6.2 AND/OR Dataflow Graphs

As has been illustrated above, derivation of inequalities between variables from given predicate inequalities has two significant aspects:

- to achieve a bound on the size of *any* out-variable, it is necessary to consider *all* variables occurring on in-positions.
- if a variable has *several* generators, it is sufficient to consider *one*.

Such a combination of *conjunction* and *disjunction* is adequately captured by the notion of AND/OR graphs and their solution graphs (see [NIL82] or [CRE86]). AND/OR graphs are special hypergraphs. Instead of arcs connecting pairs of nodes as in ordinary graphs, there are hyperarcs connecting a parent node with several successor nodes.

6.2.1 DEFINITION: *AND/OR Graphs*

An AND/OR graph is a pair $G = (V,C)$, where V is a finite set of nodes and

$$C \subseteq V \times \bigcup_{k=1}^{n} V^k.$$

The elements of C are called k-connectors. Each k-connector is a (k+1)-tuple $(n_{io},n_{i1},...,n_{ik})$; n_{io} is called parent node, the n_{ij} $(1 \le j \le k)$ are called successor nodes. ∎

What corresponds to a solution *path*, occurring in search problems represented by ordinary graphs, is a solution *graph* in an AND/OR graph G, connecting a start node with a set of success nodes.

In the following it will be assumed that G is acyclic. This allows to define a partial order $<_{ao}$ on the nodes of G: $n_i <_{ao} n_j$ iff n_i is successor of n_j.

6.2.2 DEFINITION: *Solution Graphs in AND/OR Graphs*

Let $G = (V,E)$ be an acyclic AND/OR graph, $n \in V$ and $N \subseteq V$. A solution graph G' from the start node n to the success nodes in N is a subgraph of G which is recursively constructed as follows:

- If $n \in N$, then $G' = (\{n\}, \emptyset)$;
- otherwise, if n has an outgoing k-connector $K = (n, n_1,\ldots,n_k)$ such that there is a solution graph to N from each of n_i ($1 \leq i \leq k$), then G' consists of node n, k-connector K and the solution graphs to N from each of the nodes in $\{n_1,\ldots,n_k\}$;
- otherwise, there is no solution graph from n to N.

The next definition specifies what is needed to construct AND/OR dataflow graphs.

6.2.3 DEFINITION: *Augmented Goals*

An *augmented goal* g' is a quadruple $g' = <g,In,Out,LI_g>$ where

- g is a normalized goal with $V = var(g)$.
- $In \subseteq V$ and $Out \subseteq V$.
- LI_g is a set of linear inequalities for the predicates occurring in g containing exactly one inequality for each predicate in g.

6.2.4 DEFINITION: *AND/OR Dataflow Graphs*

Let $g' = <g,In,Out,LI_g>$ be an augmented goal with

- g   = $L_1,\ldots,L_n$.
- In   = $\{u_1,\ldots,u_m\}$.
- Out = $\{w_1,\ldots,w_k\}$.
- V   = $var(g)$.

An AND/OR dataflow graph $DFG_{g'} = (N,C)$ for g' is constructed as follows:

- *Nodes*
  - For each variable $v \in V$ there is an OR-node $v \in N$.
  - There are AND-nodes 'In' and 'Out' in N; 'Out' is the start node and 'In' the end node of $DFG_{g'}$.
  - For each literal L_i in g there is an AND-node in N.

- *Connectors:*
  - o There is a k-connector ('Out',w_1,...,w_k).
  - o For $1 \le i \le m$ there are 1-connectors (u_i,'In').
  - o Let n be the node representing some literal L in g, LI the linear inequality
     for the predicate of that literal, $V = \{v_1,...,v_k\}$ and V' the sets of variables
     occurring on the in- resp. out-positions of L w.r.t. LI. There is a k-
     connector (n, v_1,...,v_k) and for all $v' \in V'$ there is a 1-connector (v',n).
     If $V = \emptyset$, then an additional dummy-node l_v is added to N and a 1-connector
     (l_v,'In') is added to C. ∎

Note that the nodes representing variables are OR-nodes and the others are AND-nodes.
Each immediate successor of an AND-node is an OR-node, and each immediate successor
of an OR-node is an AND-node. Above, all connectors starting from OR-nodes are 1-con-
nectors.

In all examples illustrated in figure 6.2.5 the AND/OR dataflow graphs themselves are
solution graphs from *'Out'* to *'In'*. This is different for the augmented goal in example
6.1.6 where the variable Y is generated in different ways. Figure 6.2.6 shows that its
AND/OR graph has two solution graphs. This reflects the nondeterminism in the
derivation of inequalities caused by multiple generation of variables.

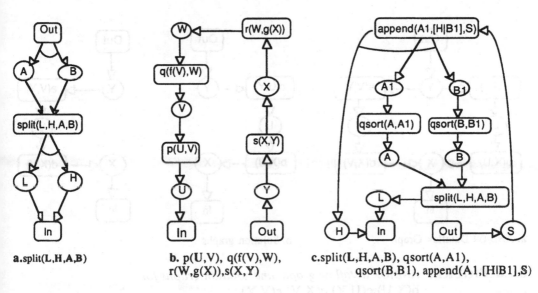

a.split(L,H,A,B)

b. p(U,V), q(f(V),W),
   r(W,g(X)),s(X,Y)

c.split(L,H,A,B), qsort(A,A1),
   qsort(B,B1), append(A1,[H|B1],S)

6.2.5 FIGURE: *Dataflow Graphs*

Figure 6.2.5 shows the dataflow graphs for some of the examples given above. In the captions, in-variables, such as **L**, are given in bold font, while out-variables, such as S, are outlined. Note that the direction of the arrows in these graphs leading from consumers to generators is opposite to the direction of dataflow. Besides being consistent with the standard notion of AND/OR graphs this is motivated by the intention to determine an upper bound for the variables which are members of *'Out'* given the variables in *'In'*. Thus these graphs can be regarded as representing some form of top down reasoning.

In the last example, the variable X, occurring in the first and third literal on in-positions, is apparently consumed twice. Both in- occurrences, however, belong to different ways to generate Y. Therefore it is possible to derive a linear inequality for that goal. In the AND/OR dataflow graph, this situation is reflected. Multiple consumption of X corresponds to the fact that in figure 6.2.6.a the node labelled X has two ingoing connectors. In each solution graph, however, it has only one.

6.2.7 DEFINITION *Admissible solution graph (ASG)*

A solution graph of an AND/OR dataflow graph is called admissible, if each OR-node has exactly one ingoing connector. ■

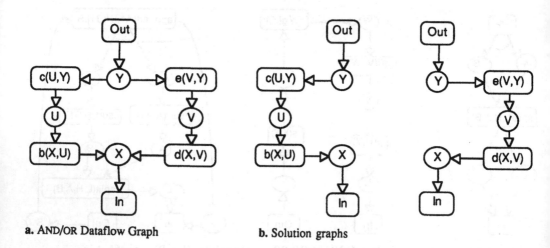

a. AND/OR Dataflow Graph   **b.** Solution graphs

6.2.6 FIGURE: *AND/OR dataflow graph and solution graphs for*
$b(X,U),c(U,Y),d(X,V),e(V,Y)$

6.3 Linear Inequalities for Augmented Goals

In this section we show that admissible solution graphs give linear inequalities for augmented goals. We start with defining weights for the nodes of an AND/OR dataflow graph.

6.3.1 DEFINITION: *Weight of AND/OR dataflow graphs*

Let $G = (N,K)$ be a subgraph of an AND/OR dataflow graph for an augmented goal g'. For some $n \in N$ its weight $\omega(n)$ is defined as follows:

- $\omega(n) = 0$ if n is an OR-node
- $\omega(n) = 0$ if n is 'In' or 'Out'
- $\omega(n) = F(L,LI)$ if L is an AND-node representing a literal L, where LI is the linear inequality for the predicate of L and F is given by def. 3.4.15.

The weight $\varpi(G)$ of G is defined by $\varpi(G) = \displaystyle\sum_{n \in N} \omega(n)$. ∎

An answer to the problem of deriving a linear inequality for variables occurring in a compound goal is given by the following theorem:

6.3.2 THEOREM: *Linear inequality for variables in a compound goal*

Let $g' = <g,\text{In},\text{Out},LI_g>$ be an augmented goal and ASG an admissible solution graph for g' with $\varpi(\text{ASG}) = c$. For every instantiation σ satisfying g validity of the linear inequalities in LI_g implies:

$$(*) \qquad \sum_{v \in \text{In}} |v\sigma| + c \geq \sum_{w \in \text{Out}} |w\sigma|.$$

PROOF: Let $g = \leftarrow L_1,\dots,L_n$. The theorem is shown by induction over n. Let $\#(\text{ASG})$ denote the number of AND-nodes different from *In* and *Out* in the admissible solution graph ASG of g'. Note that ASG being a subgraph of the AND/OR dataflow graph for g' implies that $\#(\text{ASG})$ may be strictly smaller than n.

For the base case, let $n = 1$. Then $\#(\text{ASG}) = 0$ or $\#(\text{ASG}) = 1$.

Case I: #(ASG)=0. Then ASG being a *solution graph* implies that In $\supseteq$ Out and thus ϖ(ASG) = 0. Figure 6.3.3.a illustrates this situation, where (*) is trivially true.

Case II: #(ASG)=1. Let g be $\leftarrow L_1$ and LI be the valid linear inequality for the predicate of L_1. Let M = In $\cap$ Out. ASG being a solution graph implies that In(L_1,LI) $\subseteq$ In and Out $\subseteq$ Out(L_1,LI) $\cup$ In. Admissibility of the solution graph implies that In(L_1,LI) $\cap$ M = $\emptyset$. Figure 6.3.3.b illustrates this situation. Proposition 3.4.16 then implies (*).

For the induction let n > 1 and assume that the theorem holds for augmented goals with fewer than n literals. Again two cases are possible: #(ASG) < n and #(ASG) = n.

Case III: #(ASG) < n. Then there exists a literal L_i ($1 \leq i \leq n$) which is not represented in ASG. Thus ASG is also a solution graph for an AND/OR dataflow graph of some augmented goal g" = <g*,In,Out,LIg*> with g* = $\leftarrow L_1,\ldots L_{i-1},L_{i+1},\ldots L_n$. The induction assumption then immediately implies (*).

Case IV: #(ASG)=n. This is the nontrivial case. Let OR be the set of OR-nodes of ASG and L_i be a literal of g which is minimal in the sense that OR $\cap$ Out(L_i,LI')$\subseteq$OUT. Since ASG is acyclic and #(ASG)$\geq$1 such a literal exists. Let LI' be the linear inequality for the predicate of L_i, Out_i=OR $\cap$ Out(L_i,LI') and In_i=OR $\cap$ In(L_i,LI'). Figure 6.3.4.a illustrates this situation.

Consider now the augmented goal g" which is defined as follows:

(i) g" = <g_2,In,Out',LI"> where

(ii) g_2 = $\leftarrow L_1,\ldots L_{i-1},L_{i+1},\ldots L_n$ and

(iii) Out' = (Out \ Out_i) $\cup$ In_i.

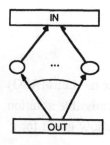

a. Case I

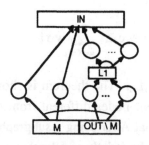

b. Case II

6.3.3 Figure: *Illustrations of Cases I and II of the proof of 6.3.2*

Construction of g" implies that there is an admissible solution graph ASG' for g". ASG' can be derived from ASG by removing L_i and the elements of Out_i and by rearranging connectors accordingly, see 6.3.4.b for illustration. Let $c = w(ASG)$ and $c' = w(ASG')$. We have $c = c' + F(L_i, LI')$. Let now σ be any instantiation satisfying g. Since g_2 has only $n-1$ literals, the induction premise can be applied, giving

(iv) $$\sum_{v \in In} |v\sigma| + c' \geq \sum_{w' \in OUT} |w'\sigma|.$$

Proposition 3.4.16 implies

(v) $$\sum_{v \in Ini} |v\sigma| + F(L_i, LI') \geq \sum_{\mu \in OUTi} |\mu\sigma|.$$

The specification of Out' in iii) then yields

(vi) $$\sum_{v \in In} |v\sigma| + c \geq \sum_{w \in OUT} |w\sigma|. \blacksquare$$

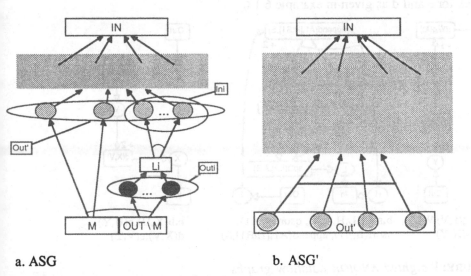

a. ASG   b. ASG'

6.3.4 Figure: *Illustrations of Case III of the proof of 6.3.2*

Theorem 6.3.2 gives us a technique of deriving inequalities relating variables in a compound goal. These are the steps:

1) check if the given goal g is normalized; if not, normalize;
2) specify the augmented goal g';
3) construct an AND/OR dataflow graph G for g';
4) construct, if possible, an admissible solution graph ASG of G;
5) compute the weight of ASG.

Figure 6.3.5 shows *weighted* admissible solution graphs for some of the examples mentioned above. Nodes with weight different from zero are labelled with their weight.

In figure 6.3.5.a the node labelled q(f(V),W) gets the weight +1 since the offset of the linear inequality for q as given in example 6.1.2 is zero, and we have | f(V) | = 1 for a term occurring at an in-position of q. The node r(W,g(X)) has weight -1 because again the offset for the linear inequality for r is zero, |g(X)| = 1, but here this term occurs at an *out*-position of r.

Figure 6.3.5.b shows the *weighted* admissible solution graph for the body of the second quicksort clause. The weight + 2 for append(A1,[H|B1],S) is caused by the list constructor which occurs at an in-position.

The weights +1 and +2 in figure 6.3.5.c are the respective offsets of the linear inequalities for e and d as given in example 6.1.6.

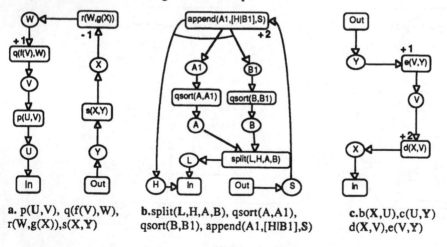

a. p(U,V), q(f(V),W),
r(W,g(X)),s(X,Y)

b.split(L,H,A,B), qsort(A,A1),
qsort(B,B1), append(A1,[H|B1],S)

c.b(X,U),c(U,Y)
d(X,V),e(V,Y)

6.3.5 FIGURE: *Weighted AND/OR dataflow graphs*

Chapter 7

A TERMINATION PROOF PROCEDURE

So far it has been assumed that linear inequalities for predicates are given. In 3.4 it has been shown how to use given inequalities to relate variable sizes in single literal goals. The last chapter has given an approach to relate variable sizes in a compound goal.

The subject of this chapter is the automatic derivation of linear inequalities for predicates. Our basic assumptions in this chapter again are that the given program is well moded, normalized and has no mutual recursion. Restriction to direct recursion is no real restriction, however. In chapter 8 we will show that every program with mutual recursion can be transformed into a semantically equivalent program without mutual recursion.

7.1 The Basic Approach

Let P be a program and $\pi \subset P$ a procedure of P defining a predicate p. Since mutual recursion is excluded, there is the partial ordering $>_\pi$ among the predicates of P which defines a directed acyclic graph (see 3.1). This graph can be traversed bottom up. Thus whenever a predicate p is processed it can be assumed that inequalities for all predicates q with $p >_\pi q$ have already been calculated.

Derivation of inequalities for predicates which are not recursive is straightforward. Recursion needs induction. The structure of an inductive proof is given by the structure of the procedure definition: the base case corresponds to the exit clauses, the inductive case to the recursive clauses.

Our task here, however, is slightly more complicated. Not only do we have to *prove* validity of given inequalities; we also have to *find* them. Thus there is also a search problem.

Searching for a valid linear inequality for a predicate p defined by a procedure π has two aspects. The first problem is which arguments are to be related. This specification can be done by a symbolic inequality (see 3.4.12). There are only finitely many symbolic inequalities for a given predicate.

Given such a symbolic inequality LI_p, the symbol γ occurring in LI_p represents an integer which is not yet fixed. Thus the second question is: for which integer γ (if any) is this inequality valid?

An answer can be given by analyzing the clauses of π. Let $C_i \in \pi$ be a clause, $C_i^0 = H$ its head and $C_i^b = g$ its body. Starting from g we can specify an augmented clause $g' = \langle g, In, Out, LI \rangle$. In and Out are the variables occurring on in- resp. out-positions of H where what is in and out is specified by LI_p. We finally get LI by adding LI_p to the set of inequalities for the predicates on which p depends.

We can now construct an AND/OR dataflow graph for g' and look for an admissible solution graph. If such a graph $ASG_{g'}$ exists and has the weight $w_{g'}$, theorem 6.3.2 allows to derive an inequality relating the elements of In and Out. Thus we can get an inequality relating the *variables* occurring on the in- resp. out-positions of H. To get an inequality relating the *terms* occurring on the respective positions we have to take function symbols occurrences into account. This requires the calculation of $F_{in}(H, LI_p)$ and $F_{out}(H, LI_p)$ (see 3.4.15). Proposition 3.4.16 then suggests to take the term $w_{g'} + F_{out}(H, LI_p) - F_{in}(H, LI_p)$ as offset of an inequality relating the in- and out-arguments of the head of C_i.

Our task is to find a value for γ which makes LI_p valid. The term

$$w_{g'} + F_{out}(H, LI_p) - F_{in}(H, LI_p)$$

derived from the analysis of the clause C_i gives a lower bound on γ. While $F_{out}(H, LI_p)$ and $F_{in}(H, LI_p)$ are integers, $w_{g'}$, the weight of an admissible solution graph for g', is a term possibly containing the symbol γ itself. This allows to derive an inequality containing a single variable, namely γ. Thus each clause of π gives a *constraint* on γ.

It remains to be checked whether the set of constraints derived from all clauses of π is consistent. If it is, the least integer satisfying it can be taken as offset of the desired inequality. We will render these informal expositions precise in the following.

7.2 γ-Constraints

The next definition specifies what is needed as input data.

7.2.1 DEFINITION: *Augmented Procedures*

An augmented procedure π' in a normalized program P without mutual recursion is a triple $<\pi,LI_p,LI>$ where

- $\pi \subset P$ is a procedure defining a predicate p.
- LI_p is a symbolic inequality for p.
- LI is a set of valid linear predicate inequalities having exactly one inequality for each predicate on which p directly depends.

Next we define weight sets for clauses. Weights will be used to derive γ-constraints. Since we can get more than one admissible solution graph for an augmented goal, we have to consider *sets* of weights.

7.2.2 DEFINITION: *Weight Set of a Clause in an Augmented Procedure*

Let $\pi' = <\pi,LI_p,LI>$ be an augmented procedure for p and $C_i \in \pi$. Let $g' = <g,In,Out,LI'>$ be an augmented clause such that

- $g = C_i^b$, i.e. g is the body of C_i.
- $H = C_i^0$, i.e. H is the head of C_i.
- In and Out are the sets of in- resp. out-variables of H wrt LI_p.
- $LI' = LI \cup \{LI_p\}$.

The weight set $w(C_i)$ is defined by

$$w(C_i) = \{w(ASG_{g'}) + F_{out}(H,LI_p) - F_{in}(H,LI_p) \mid ASG_{g'} \text{ is an admissible solution}$$
graph for g' and $w(ASG_{g'})$ does not contain the symbol '∞'$\}$ ∎

With the last restriction we exclude those admissible solution graphs which refer to inequalities having '∞' as offset. If no such graphs can be found, $w(C_i)$ is empty. This corresponds to an unsatisfiable γ-constraint set to be defined next.

7.2.3 DEFINITION: γ-Constraint Sets for Clauses

Let $\pi' = <\pi,LI_p,LI>$ be an augmented procedure for p and $C_i \in \pi$. The γ-constraint set $c_\gamma(C_i)$ is defined as follows:

(i) If $w(C_i) = \emptyset$, then $c_\gamma(C_i) = \{false\}$.

(ii) otherwise $c_\gamma(C_i) = \{w'(\Delta) \mid \Delta \in w(C_i)\}$, where $w'(\Delta)$ is defined as follows:

(a) If Δ is an integer, then $w'(\Delta) \equiv \gamma \geq \Delta$.

(b) If $\Delta = \gamma + n$, where n is an integer, then $w'(\Delta) \equiv true$ if $n \leq 0$, and $w'(\Delta) \equiv false$ otherwise.

(c) If $\Delta = k * \gamma + n$, where k and n are integers and $k > 1$, then
$$w'(\Delta) \equiv \gamma \leq \frac{n}{1-k}$$ ∎

Thus the elements of $c_\gamma(C_i)$ are 'true', 'false' or inequalities having γ on their left side.

7.2.4 DEFINITION: γ-Constraint Sets for Procedures

Let $\pi' = <\pi,LI_p,LI>$ be an augmented procedure for p and $\pi = \{C_1,...,C_n\}$. A γ-constraint set $p_\gamma(\pi')$ for π' is defined by

$$p_\gamma(\pi') = \bigcup_{i=1}^{n} \{c_{\gamma i}\}, \text{ where } c_{\gamma i} \in c_\gamma(C_i).$$ ∎

Please note that there may be more than one γ-constraint set for an augmented procedure.

An augmented procedure can be regarded as implicit specification of a problem which is made explicit by γ-constraint sets. The problem is for which integer the given symbolic inequality is valid. Such an integer can be viewed as a solution to this problem.

7.2.5 DEFINITION: *Solution of an Augmented Procedure*

An integer c is a solution of an augmented procedure π' if there exists a γ-constraint set $c_\gamma(\pi')$ which is satisfied by c. An integer c is called optimal solution of π' if for all solutions c' of π' the inequality $c \leq c'$ holds. ∎

According to the notions defined above, such a solution is derived as follows:

- Start with an augmented procedure π' for some procedure definition π.
- For all clauses C_i of π do the following:
  - Construct an augmented goal g' from the body of C_i according to def. 7.2.2 and an AND/OR dataflow graph DFG for g'. Find admissible solution graphs for DFG in order to calculate the weight set $w(C_i)$, which is a set of terms of the form $k * \gamma + n$, where k and n are integers and $k \geq 0$.
  - From the weight set $w(C_i)$ derive the constraint set $c_\gamma(C_i)$ according to def. 7.2.3.
- Derive a constraint set $p_\gamma(\pi')$ for π' by taking exactly one element from each of the $c_\gamma(C_i)$. Calculate a solution for $p_\gamma(\pi')$ as follows:
  - If $p_\gamma(\pi')$ contains the element 'false', stop: there is no solution.
  - If 'true' is contained in $p_\gamma(\pi')$ it can be eliminated.
  - The remaining elements are inequalities of the form $\gamma \geq \ldots$ or $\gamma \leq \ldots$, thus specifying an interval on the set of integers. If this interval is not empty, every integer in it is a solution of $p_\gamma(\pi')$.

We are now ready to state the following theorem which essentially says that such a solution to an augmented procedure gives a valid inequality:

7.2.6 THEOREM: *Valid Linear Inequalities for Predicates*

Let $\pi' = \langle \pi, LI_p, LI \rangle$ be an augmented procedure for a predicate p in a program P where LI has the form:

$$\sum_{i \in I} p_i + \gamma \geq \sum_{j \in J} p_j.$$

Let c be a solution for π'. Then the inequality

$$\sum_{i \in I} p_i + c \geq \sum_{j \in J} p_j$$

is valid.

PROOF: Assume that p has arity m. We have to show that for every $L = p(t_1,\ldots,t_m) \in M_P$ the following holds:

$$(*) \qquad \sum_{i \in I} |t_i| + c \geq \sum_{j \in J} |t_j|.$$

The proof is by induction on the number of occurrences of clauses of π in a forward chaining derivation of L by the T_P-operator. Consider the clause C_i. Let $H = p(s_1,\ldots,s_m)$ be the head of C_i and σ an instantiation such that $H\sigma = L$. Let $F_{in} = F_{in}(H,LI)$ and $F_{out} = F_{out}(H,LI)$. The existence of a solution for π' implies that $w(C_i) \neq \varnothing$. Let Δ be the element of $w(C_i)$ that has been used to derive c, and let ASG be the admissible solution graph used to derive Δ. Def. 7.2.2 implies that Δ is a term of the form

$$(**) \qquad \Delta = k*\gamma + n.$$

There are three cases to discuss separately: $k = 0$, $k = 1$, $k > 1$.

$k = 0$: ASG has no occurrence of an AND-node corresponding to a p-literal. In this case only *one* application of a clause of π, namely C_i, has to be considered. This is the basic case. Rewrite $(**)$ as $\Delta = 0*\gamma + n' + F_{out} - F_{in}$, with $n = n' + F_{out} - F_{in}$. Now by theorem 6.3.2 n', the weight of ASG, is an offset of an inequality relating the variables occurring on the in- and out-positions of H, respectively. This implies

$$\sum_{i \in I} |s_i\theta| + n \geq \sum_{j \in J} |s_j\theta|$$

for all instantiations θ satisfying the body of C_i. Now def. 7.2.3.a implies $c \geq n$ which yields $(*)$.

$k = 1$: ASG has exactly one occurrence of a p-literal. This is an inductive case. It roughly corresponds to linear recursion. Rewrite $(**)$ as $\Delta = \gamma + n' + F_{out} - F_{in}$. The weight of ASG is $\gamma + n'$. Induction assumption and theorem 6.3.2 imply that $c + n'$ is the offset of a linear inequality relating the variables occurring on the in- resp. out-positions of H. This implies

$$\sum_{i \in I} |s_i\theta| + c + n' + F_{out} - F_{in} \geq \sum_{j \in J} |s_j\theta|$$

for all instantiations θ satisfying the body of C_i. Since $w'(\Delta)$ must be true, $n' + F_{out} - F_{in} \leq 0$ by 7.2.3.b. This implies $(*)$.

$k > 1$: ASG has more than one occurrence of p-literals. This again is an inductive case. It corresponds to nonlinear recursion. Rewrite (**) as
$\Delta = k * \gamma + n' + F_{out} - F_{in}$. The weight of ASG is $k * \gamma + n'$. The same considerations as in the last case give

$$\sum_{i \in I} |s_i \theta| + k * c + n' + F_{out} - F_{in} \geq \sum_{j \in J} |s_j \theta|$$

for all instantiations θ satisfying the body of C_i. Def. 7.2.3.c now implies that

$$c \leq \frac{n' + F_{out} - F_{in}}{1 - k} \quad \text{which yields (**).} \blacksquare$$

Next we give two examples how to use the theorem given above.

7.2.7 EXAMPLE: *Linear Inequality for Qsort*

The quicksort example has already been used for illustration in 6.1.1. We repeat the definition of qsort here and show admissible solution graphs for both of its clauses. Linear inequalities for split and append have been given in 6.1.3.

q_1: qsort([],[]).
q_2: qsort([H|L],S) ← split(L,H,A,B), qsort(A,A1), qsort(B,B1),
append(A1,[H|B1],S).

We start with the symbolic inequality

LI_q: qsort$_1$ + γ ≥ qsort$_2$.

Clause q_1 has an empty body and no variable occurrences in its head. The admissible solution graph in this case is trivial: It has only the AND-nodes In and Out, representing empty sets, and a dummy node.

Obviously $w(ASG_1) = 0$. We further have $F_{out}(qsort([],[]),LI_q) = 0$ and $F_{in}(qsort([],[]),LI_q) = 0$, so by def. 7.2.2 $w(q_1) = \{0\}$. According to def. 7.2.3 we get the γ-constraint $c_\gamma(q_1) = \{\gamma \geq 0\}$.

As 7.2.8.b shows $w(ASG_2) = 2 * \gamma + 2$. We further have $F_{in}(qsort([H|L],S),LI_q) = 2$ and $F_{out}(qsort([H|L],S),LI_q) = 0$, thus $w(q_2) = \{2 * \gamma + 0\}$. This gives the γ-constraint

$$c_\gamma(q_2) = \{ \gamma \leq \frac{0}{1 - 2} \} = \{ \gamma \leq 0 \}$$

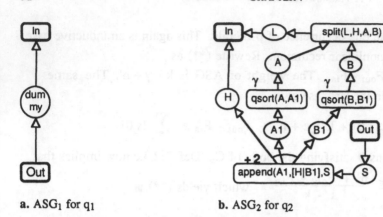

a. ASG_1 for q_1 **b.** ASG_2 for q_2

7.2.8 FIGURE: *Admissible solution graphs for qsort-clauses*

Thus for the qsort procedure we get the γ-constraint set $\{\gamma \geq 0, \gamma \leq 0\}$ which has 0 as unique solution. Theorem 7.2.6 then implies

$$\text{qsort}_1 \geq \text{qsort}_2 \quad \blacksquare$$

7.2.9 EXAMPLE: *The Procedure Mult*

m_1:   mult(0,Y,0).
m_2:   mult(s(X),Y,Z) $\leftarrow$ mult(X,Y,Z1),add(Z1,Y,Z).
a_1:   add(0,Y_1,Y_2) $\leftarrow$ equal(Y_1,Y_2).
a_2:   add(s(X),Y,s(Z)) $\leftarrow$ add(X,Y,Z).

We start with:

$\text{add}_1 + \text{add}_2 + 0 \geq \text{add}_3$ and
$\text{mult}_1 + \text{mult}_2 + \gamma \geq \text{mult}_3$

Figure 7.2.10 shows AND/OR dataflow graphs for both clauses of mult. The first clause, which is a unit clause, has a variable, namely 'Y', which occurs on an in- but not on an out-position: multiplication with zero is always zero and does not depend on the second argument. In the AND/OR dataflow graph for m_1 (7.2.10.a) the OR-node representing 'Y' therefore has one outgoing but no ingoing connector. Since this node is not - reachable from 'Out' it does not appear in the admissible solution graph for m_1 as illustrated in 7.2.10.b. This graph has weight zero, and the γ-constraint derived from the first clause for mult is $\gamma \geq 0$.

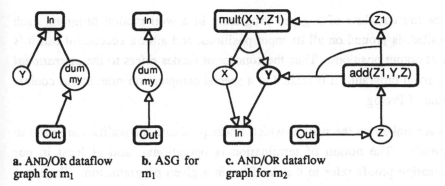

a. AND/OR dataflow graph for m_1 **b.** ASG for m_1 **c.** AND/OR dataflow graph for m_2

7.2.10 FIGURE: *AND/OR dataflow graphs for mult*

Figure 7.2.10.c shows the AND/OR dataflow graph for m_2. This graph itself is a solution graph for 'In'. The OR-node representing 'Y', however, has two ingoing connectors.

This solution graph is therefore not admissible. Variable 'Y' is consumed twice in the body of $mult_2$; it occurs on an in- position of mult(X,Y,Z1) and on an in-position of add(Z1,Y,Z). Therefore no linear inequality for mult can be derived. This is no surprise, however, since the relation between the mult arguments is not linear.

The last example demonstrates that admissibility of a solution graph of an AND/OR dataflow graphs is indeed crucial to derive linear inequalities from given ones. Multiple consumption of variables may lead - although not necessarily, as a later example will show - to a nonlinear size relation between input and output.

7.3 Linear Predicate Inequalities and Modes

Although in termination proofs modes and predicate inequalities are closely linked together, they are independent concepts.

Linear predicate inequalities refer to literals which are in the minimal Herbrand model of a given program. The elements of the minimal Herbrand model are ground atomic formula by definition. Predicate inequalities approximatively compare the sizes of their argument terms. Thus the concept of linear predicate inequalities is *declarative*. No reference to the operational semantics and a special evaluation strategy is needed.

Modes describe the dataflow of a given program. In a well moded program, each literal, when called, is ground on all its input positions, and after a successful call it is ground on all its output positions. Thus the concept of modes refers to the *operational* semantics of a given program. It is related to a special computation rule, in our context the standard rule of Prolog.

Both concepts are linked by the way in which linear predicate inequalities are used in termination proofs. The notion of termination is operational, and at least in our approach termination proofs refer to the dataflow in a given program, too. The arguments of recursive procedures which are expected to decrease at each recursive call have to be be ground each time the procedure is called. Therefore in the context of termination proofs arguments on the larger side of an inequality for a predicate p should be input arguments while the arguments on its smaller side should be output arguments, where the terms 'input' and 'output' refer to the mode of p.

There is some affinity between modes and AND/OR dataflow graphs which is explicated in the following.

7.3.1 DEFINITION: *Mode Covering*

An inequality LI_p is *covered by* a mode d_p for a predicate p, if $d_p(i) = $ '+' for all $i \in Pos_{in}(LI_p)$ and $d_p(i) = $ '-' for all $i \in Pos_{out}(LI_p)$. This covering is strong, if $d_p(i) = $ '-' implies $i \in Pos_{out}(LI_p)$ and $d_p(i) = $ '+' implies $i \in Pos_{in}(LI_p)$.

7.3.2 THEOREM: *AND/OR dataflow graphs and mode covering*

Let $\pi' = <\pi,LI_p,LI>$ be an augmented procedure in a well moded pro-gram P and M a set of modes for the predicates in $\{p\} \cup \{q| p \underset{\pi}{\rightarrow} q\}$. If each linear inequality in $\{LI_p\} \cup LI$ is covered by the corresponding mode in M, then all AND/OR dataflow graphs for the clauses of π are *acyclic*. If all coverings are strong, then these AND/OR dataflow graphs have solution graphs.

PROOF: Let $C_i = L_0 \leftarrow L_1,...,L_n \in \pi$ and let the augmented goal g' be specified as in 7.2.2. Let $LI' = \{LI_p\} \cup LI$. If the linear inequalities in LI' are covered by the modes in M, the and-or-dataflow graph DFG_i for g' and the literal dependency graph LDG_i for C_i are related to each other in the following way: If there is a k-connector $<L_i,\{v_1,...,v_r,...,v_k\}>$ and a 1-connector $<v_r,L_j>$ for i,j > 0 in DFG_i, then there is an edge $<L_j,L_i>$ labelled V in G_c and $v_r \in V$. Since P is well moded there is a partial order on the body literals of c, so we can have no cycle in DFG_i containing more than one AND-node. Since a clause in an augmented procedure is assumed to be normalized, we have no cycles at all.

If the covering is strong, we further have: If there is an edge $<L_j,L_i>$ labelled V in G_c, $v \in V$ and $v \in In(L_i,LI')$, then there is some k-connector $<L_i,\{v_1,...,v,...,v_k\}>$ and a 1-connector $<v,L_j>$ in $ASG_{g'}$. Since the the literal dependency graph LDG_i for C_i is full and all out- / in-variables in the head of C_i are in the start / end node of DFG_i, the existence of a solution graph for LDG_i is guaranteed. ∎

7.3.3 DEFINITION: *Canonical Inequalities for well moded Programs*

Let P be a well moded program and LI a set of linear inequalities for predicates in P. LI is called canonical if all its elements are strongly covered by the respective modes ∎

7.4 Termination Proofs Using Predicate Inequalities

We now discuss a general algorithm applying the techniques described so far.

7.4.1 DEFINITION: *Safe Procedures with Local Variables*

Let P be a well moded program and $\pi \subset P$ a procedure definition for a predicate p. Let $\mathfrak{S}$ be a set of input indices of p (w.r.t. the mode of p), $C_i = L_{i,0} \leftarrow L_{i,1},...,L_{i,j},...,L_{i,m} \in \pi$ with a recursive literal $L_{i,j}$, $L_{i,0} = p(t_1,...,t_n)$, and $L_{i,j} = p(s_1,...,s_n)$. An AND/OR dataflow graph $DFG_{i,j}$ for $L_{i,j}$ w.r.t. $\mathfrak{S}$ corresponds to the augmented goal $g' = <g,In,Out,LI>$, where

- $g = L_{i,1},...,L_{i,j-1}$
- $In = \bigcup_{i \in \mathfrak{S}} var(t_i)$ and $Out = \bigcup_{i \in \mathfrak{S}} var(s_i)$

- LI is a set having exactly one valid linear inequality for each predicate occurring in g.

Let $F_1 = \sum_{i \in \mathfrak{S}} |t_i|$ and $F_2 = \sum_{i \in \mathfrak{S}} |s_i|$. $L_{i,j}$ is called safe w.r.t. $\mathfrak{S}$ if there exists an admissible solution graph for $DFG_{i,j}$ with weight c such that $c + F_2 - F_1 < 0$. It is safe *in a weak sense* if $c + F_2 - F_1 \leq 0$.

The procedure π is called safe w.r.t. $\mathfrak{S}$ if all its recursive literals $L_{i,j}$ are safe w.r.t. $\mathfrak{S}$. A procedure π for a predicate p is called safe if there exists a set of input indices $\mathfrak{S}_p$ such that π is safe w.r.t. $\mathfrak{S}_p$. In this case $\mathfrak{S}_p$ is called a set of safe indices for π resp. p. If $\mathfrak{S}_p$ is the set of input indices w.r.t. the mode of p it is called the canonical set of input indices. ∎

7.4.2 THEOREM: *Safe Predicates have no Recursive Loops*

Let P be a well moded program without mutual recursion and $\pi \subset P$ be a procedure definition for a safe predicate p. Let G be a single literal goal which is ground on all input positions. Then the proof tree T for (P,G), constructed according to the Prolog computation rule, has no recursive loop for p.

PROOF: By contradiction. Assume that $L_0, L_1, \ldots$ is a recursive loop for p with $L_0 = G$. Because of def. 4.3.3 there is some $i \geq 0$ such that all L_j with $j \geq i$ are p-literals. Since P is well moded and G is ground on all input positions, all literals L_j are ground on all input positions. Now assume that for any $j \geq i$

$$\begin{aligned} L_j &= \leftarrow p(t_1,\ldots,t_n) \text{ and} \\ L_{j+1} &= \leftarrow p(s_1,\ldots,s_n). \end{aligned}$$

Since L_j is parent node of L_{j+1} in T, by 4.1.1 there must be a clause $C \in \pi$, some k and a substitution σ such that

$$\begin{aligned} C &= A \leftarrow B_1,\ldots,B_k,\ldots,B_m, \\ A\sigma &= p(t_1,\ldots,t_n), \\ B_k\sigma &= p(s_1,\ldots,s_n), \\ A &= p(t_1',\ldots,t_n'), \\ B_k &= p(s_1',\ldots,s_n'). \end{aligned}$$

Since p is safe, there is a set of safe indices $\mathfrak{S}_p$. Let g' be the augmented goal <g,In,Out,LI> where $g = \leftarrow B_1,\ldots,B_{k-1}$ and In, Out and LI are defined as in def. 7.4.1. According to this definition there is an admissible solution graph for the AND/OR dataflow graph for g' with weight c. Since L_{j+1} is an inner node and T is constructed according to the Prolog computation rule, the substitution σ is a computed answer for the goal $B_1,\ldots,B_{k-1}$. Since P is well-moded, $(B_1,\ldots,B_{k-1})\sigma$ is ground. We therefore have

(i) $\displaystyle\sum_{v\in In} |v\sigma| + c \geq \sum_{w\in Out} |w\sigma|$ by theorem 6.3.2.

Now let $F_1 = \displaystyle\sum_{i\in S} |t_i'|$ and $F_2 = \displaystyle\sum_{i\in S} |s_i'|$.

This gives

(ii) $\displaystyle\sum_{i\in S} |t_i'\sigma| + c + F_2 - F_1 \geq \sum_{i\in S} |s_i'\sigma|$

which implies

(iii) $\displaystyle\sum_{i\in S} |t_i| > \sum_{i\in S} |s_i|$

since by 7.4.1 $c + F_2 - F_1 < 0$, and for $i=1,\ldots,n$ $t_i'\sigma = t_i$ and $s_i'\sigma = s_i$.

The last inequality shows that the sequence L_i, L_{i+1}, ... is strictly decreasing for some well founded ordering, contrary to the assumption that it is infinite. ■

7.4.3 Theorem: *Terminating Queries based on Safe Predicates*

Let $\Pi = (P, \leftarrow p(t_1,\ldots,t_n))$ be a well moded, queried program without mutual recursion and $Q = \{q \mid p \underset{\pi}{\Rightarrow}^* q\}$. If all elements of Q are safe, then G terminates.

PROOF: According to 4.2.1 we have to show that there is a finite depth for all proof trees for $(P,G\theta)$.

We first show that all proof trees are finite. Assume the contrary. Then there exists a literal q which has a recursive loop in some proof tree T and $p \underset{\pi}{\Rightarrow}^* q$ since p is the predicate of the initial query. But this contradicts the assumption that all elements of Q are safe.

Assume now that there is no finite depth for the proof trees for Π, that is, for all $n > 0$ there is a recursive branch L_0, $L_1,\ldots,$ $L_n,\ldots$ with length $> n$ in some proof tree T. Let now n_1 be the length of the longest acyclic path starting from p in the predicate dependency graph of G. Since P is free of mutual recursion we can fix a predicate q such that all L_j with $j > n_1$ are q-literals. Now consider L_m where $m = 1 + n_1$. Since q is safe there is some safe set of input indices $\mathfrak{I}$ for q.

Let $L_m = q(s_1,\ldots,s_k)$ and $n_2 = \sum_{i \in \mathfrak{I}} |s_i|$. Inequality (iii) in the proof of 7.4.2 then implies that the length of the path considered cannot exceed $n_1 + n_2 + 1$, contradicting the assumption that there is no such bound. ∎

The last theorem can be generalized to a statement that captures all well moded queries to a given program:

7.4.4 COROLLARY: *Terminating Programs*

Let P be a well moded program such that all its predicates are safe. Then each well moded query terminates.

PROOF: Corollary 7.4.4 is a direct consequence of theorem 7.4.3.

7.4.5 ALGORITHM: *Automatic Termination Proof (Weak Version)*

INPUT: A normalized, well moded program P without mutual recursion

(1) Construct the Predicate Dependency Graph G_π for P, eliminate its loops, and traverse it bottom up to get a list LoP: $[p_1,\ldots,p_n]$ of predicates of P.

(2) Let $\{LI_1,\ldots,LI_n\}$ be a set of canonical symbolic linear inequalities for P such that inequality LI_i corresponds to predicate p_i

(3) Process the list of predicates LoP sequentially as follows:

    (a) Let π_i be the procedure defining p_i and $\pi'_i = <\pi_i, LI_i, LI_{dep(i)}>$, where $LI_{dep(i)} \subseteq \{LI_1',\ldots,LI_{i-1}'\}$ has valid linear inequalities for all predicates $q \neq p$ on which p directly depends.

    (b) If π_i' has a solution, let c_i be an optimal solution for π_i'. Replace γ in LI_i by c_i to get LI_i'. Otherwise replace γ in LI_i by '∞' to get LI_i'.

    (c) Check whether or not the canonical set of input indices $\mathfrak{I}_{p_i}$ for π_i is safe. If not, answer

> "A query calling procedure π_i may not terminate since π_i is unsafe for the
> canonical set of input indices."
> and stop.

(4)   Answer: "All well moded queries for P terminate".

It is a direct consequence of corollary 7.4.4 that the answers given by this algorithm are correct.

It ought to be stressed however that for the input program P the following conditions have to be satisfied:

(i)   P is normalized.

(ii)   P is free of mutual recursion.

(iii)   P is well moded.

Transformation of some program P_0 into a semantically equivalent program P_1 which meets the first requirement is straightforward. As has been pointed out in the diploma thesis of Hösterey, such a transformation has an interesting side effect: the normal Prolog interpreter without occur check will produce no cyclic terms evaluating such a program if the 'equal'-predicate used in this transformation implements unification correctly, i.e., with occur check (see [HOE88]).

Transformation of program P_1 into a semantically equivalent program P_2 without mutual recursion is always possible, too. We will discuss such a procedure in the next chapter.

Well-modedness, however, can not always be achieved. As discussed in 3.2, goal reordering may be necessary. But even then there are programs having no annotations which would make them well-moded. If a proper annotation exists, well-modedness can be achieved rather efficiently by well known techniques (see [MEL87] and [DEW88] for instance).

Thus it can be assumed that the satisfaction of the three conditions mentioned above is checked or if possible achieved by a preprocessor. Algorithm 7.4.5 then has to be applied to the transformed program, and, in fact, tells about the transformed program. This distinction has to be made since for instance goal reordering, employed to achieve well modedness, might transform a nonterminating program in a terminating one.

Algorithm 7.4.5 is weaker than it could be. The reason is that only *canonical* inequalities are considered. The *qsort* procedure is an example which shows that it is not sufficient to consider canonical inequalities to achieve a termination proof. The admissible solution graph ASG_2 in figure 7.2.8 assumes that for *split* the inequality

$\qquad$ (1) $\qquad$ $split_1 \geq split_3 + split_4$.

is given. This inequality is not canonical, however, since *split* has the mode

$\qquad\qquad$ mode(split(+,+,-,-)).

Inequality (1) subsumes the following canonical inequality (2) for *split*, which is weaker:

$\qquad$ (2) $\qquad$ $split_1 + split_2 \geq split_3 + split_4$.

Figure 7.4.7 shows the AND/OR dataflow graph for the second qsort-clause which corresponds to inequality (2). It has no admissible solution graph. The AND/OR dataflow graph is itself a solution graph, but it is not admissible since H has two ingoing connectors.

Algorithm 7.4.5 can be refined by considering *all* symbolic inequalities for p_i which are covered by the mode of p_i instead of restricting attention to the single inequality which is strongly covered by the predicates' mode. This may result in having several valid linear inequalities instead of a single one. Before giving this refinement we need the following definition:

7.4.6 DEFINITION: *Derived Set of Inequalities*

Let P be a normalized, well moded program without mutual recursion and $\pi \subset P$ be the procedure definition for p. Let LI be a set of *valid linear inequalities* for the predicates in $Q = \{q \mid p \underset{\pi}{\Rightarrow}^* q \text{ and } q \neq p\}$ and LI_p^* be the set of *symbolic* inequalities for p which are covered by the mode of p. Let M be the set

$\quad$ M $=$ $\{S \mid S$ is an optimal solution for $\langle \pi, \Lambda_p, \Lambda \rangle$ where $\Lambda_p \in LI_p^*$ and $\Lambda \subseteq LI$
$\qquad\qquad$ such that for each predicate in Q Λ has exactly one inequality$\}$

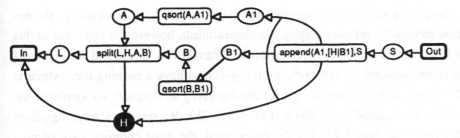

7.4.7 FIGURE: *AND/OR dataflow graph for the second qsort clause corresponding to inequality (2)*

and N' be the greatest subset of M such that there is no pair of different elements α and β such that α is stronger than β. Let Out be the set of out-positions of p and $N = N' \cup \{`\infty \geq \sum_{i \in \text{Out}} p_i'\}$. Then N is called the set of valid linear inequalities derived for $\pi \subset P$ with LI. We write

$$\pi \vdash\!\frac{\text{LI}}{P}\!N.$$

7.4.8 ALGORITHM: *Automatic Termination Proof (Refined Version)*

INPUT: A normalized, well moded program P without mutual recursion

(1) Construct the Predicate Dependency Graph G_π for P, eliminate its loops, and traverse it bottom up to get the list LoP: $[p_1,...,p_n]$ of the predicates of P.

(2) Let $\text{LI}_0^* = \varnothing$.

(3) Process the list of predicates LoP sequentially as follows:

    (a) Calculate N_i such that $\pi_i \vdash\!\frac{\text{LI}_{i-1}}{P}\!N_i$.

    (b) Let $\text{LI}_i^* = \text{LI}_{i-1}^* \cup N_i$.

    (c) Check whether or not a set of safe indices $\Im_{p_i}$ for π_i exists.
    If not, answer
    "A query calling procedure π_i may not terminate since π_i is unsafe."
    and stop.

(4) Answer: *"All well moded queries for P terminate"*.

Both algorithms 7.4.5 and 7.4.8 are nondeterministic on the clause level due to the necessity to find admissible solution graphs. Nondeterminism, however, is restricted to this level. Thus if the numbers of the variables and the literals in a clause and the arities of the predicates are bounded by constants, both algorithms have a running time which is linear in the length of the program. Due to the necessity to consider all symbolic inequalities which are covered by modes and to check all index sets for safety, algorithm 7.4.8 needs more time than 7.4.5. On the other hand, the most common case of programs where no variable is generated more than once is of special interest. *"Generally functional programs"*, which have been studied by Barbuti and Martelli (see [BAM87]), have this property. The *uniqueness* property, introduced by Ullman and van Gelder (see [ULG88]), also implies that no variable is generated more than once. In this case, the identification of an admissible solution graph is also deterministic.

We now look at the time complexity of algorithm 7.4.5 for this common case in more detail. Suppose we have as input a program P in which no variable is generated more than once. Let n be the number of clauses and k the maximum of the textual length of the clauses in P. $O(n*k)$ time suffices for constructing the predicate dependency graph G_π for P and the list LoP in step (1). The same is true for the construction of the set of symbolic linear inequalities in step (2). To perform step (3a) and (3b), an AND/OR dataflow graphs has to be constructed for each clause, and an admissible solution graph has to be identified. Since each variable has exactly one outgoing connector, no search is needed, and there is at most one admissible solution graph for each clause. $O(k^2)$ time suffices to construct the AND/OR dataflow graph and - if possible - the admissible solution graph for one clause. Finding the optimal solution for each π_i' can be done by interval intersection, i.e. in linear time. Thus for the derivation of inequalities in (3a) and (3b) we get time complexity $O(n*k^2)$. For the termination proofs it has to be checked in (3c) whether the canonical sets of input indices are safe. To this end all recursive literals have to be considered, and for each of them AND/OR dataflow graphs and admissible solution graphs have to be constructed. If r is the maximal number of recursive literals in a clause, $O(n*r*k^2)$ suffices for doing this job. This means that the time complexity of algorithm 7.4.5 for the case of programs in which no variables are generated more than once is $O(n*r*k^2)$.

7.5 The Bounded Term Size Property

According to def. 4.5.1 well moded programs have the bounded term size property if no subgoal in an SLD-derivation has an argument with length greater than $f(n)$ provided that no argument of the top-level goal has length greater than n for some function f. Such programs are interesting since theorem 4.5.11 shows that their OLDT refutations are finite. In this section we will give a sufficient condition for the bounded term size property.

7.5.1 PROPOSITION: *Safe predicates and bounded recursion*

If all predicates of a well moded program P are safe, then P has the bounded term size property.

PROOF: According to 7.4.4 P terminates for well moded queries.

Safety of predicates implies that some input arguments are *strictly* decreasing at recursive calls. We now show how this restriction can be weakened.

7.5.2 DEFINITION: *Restrained Predicates*

An n-ary predicate p of a well moded program P is restrained if it is safe or if the following holds:

(i)   There is a valid linear inequality LI_p for p such that $o(LI_p) \in Z$ and $Pos_{in}(LI_p) \cup Pos_{out}(LI_p) = \{1,...,n\}$.

(ii) Let $\mathfrak{S} = Pos_{in}(LI_p)$. All recursive literals L_{ij} occurring in the definition of p are safe in a weak sense w.r.t. $\mathfrak{S}$ (see def. 7.4.1).

(iii) All output arguments of each of the L_{ij} are variables which do not occur on the left of L_{ij}. (This can easily be achieved by program transformation)

The program P is restrained if all its predicates are restrained. ∎

7.5.3 THEOREM: *Restrained programs have the bounded term size property.*

PROOF: Let P be a restrained program and G a well moded goal for P. Let L be an n-ary p-literal occurring in a proof tree T for G. Since P is well moded, evaluation of G is data driven. Therefore L is ground on all its input positions. Two cases are possible:

(a)   The predicate p is safe. Then evaluation of L terminates, and there is a bound on the arguments occurring in derivations of L.

(b)   The predicate p is unsafe. If evaluation of L terminates, we are ready. Now assume that there is a recursive loop for p. Since p is restrained, (ii) in 7.5.2 implies that the input arguments in this branch at least do not increase. Note that these arguments are ground. (i) and (iii) together imply that there is also an upper bound on the output arguments.

Since for both cases existence of bounds can be derived, induction on the number of predicates occurring in P proves the theorem. ∎

7.6 A Self-Application Experiment

A loop checking tool based on algorithm 7.4.5 has been implemented in Quintus Prolog. In order to find out whether or not our technique can cope with non-trivial problems we have made a self-application experiment. We took the program - let us call it LCT (Loop Checking Tool) - and had it check whether or not LCT is safe. The result is as follows: LCT, which has a size of 50 Kbytes roughly corresponding to 24 pages source code, was able to derive inequalities and to verify termination of all its procedures except for three. Running on a SUN 4 in Quintus Prolog, this took 105 seconds. In the following we discuss the problems we observed during this experiment and discuss the reason why LCT failed in the three cases mentioned.

Algorithm 7.4.5 assumes that the input program is well-moded, normalized, and free of mutual recursion. The first condition is a problem since LCT operates on clauses which are not ground in most cases. Handling object level variables on a meta-level is a general problem of meta-programming in logic programming. According to a proposal of Lloyd and Hill (see [LLH88]), this problem can be dealt with in a clean way by representing object level variables by meta-level constants. These constants are assumed to be of a special type 'variable', and the built-in predicate 'var' is used to check for this type. Accordingly it can be assumed that the program, which is given as the input of LCT, is ground.

LCT makes use of a few built-in, meta-logical predicates. One of them is the 'var'-predicate mentioned above, another one the 'univ'-predicate '=..'. One way to use '=..' is to decompose terms, another way is to construct terms. In LCT we use it only in the first way, for instance in order to calculate $F(L, LI_p)$ (see definition 3.4.15).

If X is bound to a term which is not a variable, $X =.. L$ means "L is the list consisting of the functor of X followed by the arguments of X". We give an example:

$$\leftarrow foo(x,y,z) =.. L \qquad \text{gives}$$

$$L = [foo,x,y,z].$$

In the context of termination proofs we would like to have a linear inequality of the form

$$LI_{=..}: \quad \text{'univ'}_1 + c \geq \text{'univ'}_2$$

which corresponds to the decomposing mode of univ. Validity of this inequality requires that the size of the structure which is input of '=..' is - apart from a constant c - greater or equal than the size of the structure to which it is decomposed.

Whether or not such an inequality exists depends on the norm which is used. The inequality $LI_{=..}$ is not valid for the n-norm. Applied to the example above we have $| foo(x,y,z) |_n = 3$ and $| [foo,x,y,z] |_n = 8$. Therefore we use a different norm which is equal to the n-norm except for the list-constructor '.' which has weight one. Integers are regarded as constants and have weight zero. The latter allows to give an inequality for the 'is'-predicate which evaluates arithmetic expressions and is sufficient for our purpose. In other cases it might be a better idea to use arithmetical predicates like 'plus' and 'times' directly instead of referring to 'is'.

Instead of the univ-predicate itself we use a predicate '=...' which is defined as follows:

```
L =... [.|L]    ←    list(L).
T =... L        ←    not list(T), T=..L.
list([]).
list([H|T])     ←    list(T).
```

That is, our modified univ-predicate treats lists in a special way and operates like univ if applied to structured terms which are not lists. If we denote this new predicate by univ', the following inequality is valid:

LI$_{=...}$:   univ'$_1$ + 1 ≥ univ'$_2$.

We also use the bagof predicate in order to collect sets of solutions.

The goal

$$\leftarrow \text{bagof}(X,G,L)$$

will produce the list L of all solutions for X such that the single-literal goal G is satisfied. Although bagof is useful for many applications, it is not first order. Like var, univ etc. bagof is a meta-logic feature of Prolog.

The concept of modes cannot be directly applied to bagof, nor does it make sense in our context to derive a linear inequality for bagof. The length of the list, to which L is bound, depends on the number of solutions which are derived for G. We can, however, state the following:

(i)   If G is called in a proper mode and the variable X occurs on an output position of G, then L is ground.

(ii) If moreover the predicate of G is safe, then ← bagof(X,G,L) terminates.

Predicate-Symbol	Mode	Inequality
=...	mode(+ =... -)	$\#_1 + 1 \geq \#_2$
var	mode(var(+))	$0 \geq 0$
is	mode(- is +)	$1 \geq \#_1$
not	mode(not +)	$0 \geq 0$
bagof	none	none

7.6.1 Table: *Linear Inequalities and Modes for Built-Ins used in LCT*
(Predicate -symbols are abbreviated by '#' in the Inequality-column)

Thus in our context bagof should be regarded as a special form which needs a special treatment in a termination proof.

LCT treats programs as if they were single modules. This means that for built-ins valid linear inequalities as well as modes are needed as additional input. Inequalities and modes for built-ins applied in LCT are given in table 7.6.1.

LCT was able to prove that its own procedures are safe except for three. The three procedures where LCT failed to prove termination are all of the same kind. The problem is to traverse a possibly cyclic graph. This problem can be specified with the bagof-predicate and the reachability relation. In the following we consider several definitions of 'reach'

7.6.2 EXAMPLE: *Reachability in Graphs*

r^1_1: reach^1(X,Y,Edges) $\leftarrow$ member([X,Y],Edges).
r^1_2: reach^1(X,Z,Edges) $\leftarrow$ member([X,Y],Edges), reach^1(Y,Z,Edges).

m_1: member(X,[X|T]).
m_2: member(X,[H|T]) $\leftarrow$ member(X,T).

Goal: $\leftarrow$ reach(U,V,Edges).

The goal is satisfied if node 'V' can be reached from node 'U' in the graph which is specified by its list of 'Edges'. This program is correct in a declarative sense. The standard Prolog interpreter does loop, however, if the graph specified by 'Edges' is cyclic. Here is an example:

$\leftarrow$ reach^1(a,N,[[x,y],[y,z],[z,x]]).

A more powerful strategy, such as OLDT, avoids these loops.

The experienced Prolog programmer normally would avoid loops by giving a definition of reach similar to the following one:

r^2_1: reach^2(X,Y,Edges,Visited) $\leftarrow$ member([X,Y],Edges).
r^2_2: reach^2(X,Z,Edges,Visited) $\leftarrow$ member([X,Y],Edges),
not member(Y,Visited),
reach^2(Y,Z,Edges,[Y|Visited]).

In this version the last argument of reach^2 is used for bookkeeping the nodes which had already been visited. Looping is prevented by the negative literal 'not member(Y,Visited)'.

The predicate reach^2 has the mode(reach(+,-,+,+)). It always terminates when called in this mode. LCT, however, is unable to verify termination. None of the input arguments of reach^2 becomes smaller. Instead, the fourth argument, bound to a list of nodes which have already been visited, becomes larger. The length of this list, however, cannot exceed the number of nodes occurring in the graph represented by the second argument, and this is why reach^2 terminates.

There is another definition for reach, which allows our technique to verify termination:

r^3_1: reach^3(X,Y,Edges,Not_Visited)   ←   member([X,Y],Edges).
r^3_2: reach^3(X,Z,Edges,Not_Visited)   ←   member([X,Y],Edges),
                                                      member(Y,Not_Visited),
                                                      delete(Y,Not_Visited,V'),
                                                      reach^3(Y,Z,Edges,V').

d_1: delete(X,[X|Y],Y).
d_2: delete(X,[H|T$_1$],[H|T$_2$])   ←   delete(X,T$_1$,T$_2$).

Instead of bookkeeping the nodes which have been visited reach^3 keeps a list of nodes which have not yet been visited. The size of this list decreases at each recursive call. On the entry level, reach^3 has to be called with its last argument bound to a list of all nodes occurring in the graph to be traversed. Here is an example:

← reach(x,N,[[x,y],[y,z],[z,x]],[x,y,z]).

Thus there are several approaches to the problem given by example 7.6.2:

- reach^1 is evaluated by OLDT. Since reach^1 is restrained in the sense of 7.5.2, termination of OLDT is guaranteed by theorem 7.5.3 and 4.5.11.
- reach^3 is evaluated by Prolog. Termination is verified by LCT.

It remains to be an open question how the techniques described so far can be strengthened such that termination of reach^2 can be derived.

Chapter 8

INTEGRATION OF
UNFOLDING TECHNIQUES

In the last chapter an algorithm was presented which derives inequalities for the predicates of a given program and checks whether these predicates are safe. Derived inequalities are valid and safe predicates terminate for well moded queries. It is sufficient but not necessary for the validity of an inequality that algorithm 7.4.8 is able to derive it. As subsequent examples will illustrate, there are procedures having valid linear inequalities which alg. 7.4.8 cannot derive. There are procedures which terminate for well moded queries, but termination can not be shown with the technique described so far for some superficial reasons.

If one uses the proof technique described in [BOE87] it is not hard to show that the question, whether a linear inequality is valid, is undecidable in general. What can be done at best is to design an algorithm which derives valid linear inequalities and shows termination for a class of problems which is reasonably large from a pragmatic point of view. The aim of this chapter is to broaden the scope of the algorithm given above by program transformation. If alg. 7.4.8 fails to derive safety of the predicates of a given program P, this program is transformed to a semantically equivalent program P' by unfolding. Then P' becomes input of alg. 7.4.8. There will be several examples illustrating where transformations are useful. Cases will be identified where unfolding is able to eliminate mutual recursion. Finally we will show how the process of unfolding can be controlled, such that unfolding itself does not loop forever.

8.1 Achieving Admissibility by Unfolding

Admissible solution graphs for each of the clauses of a given predicate p are needed for the derivation of a linear inequality for p. While the existence of a solution graph is implied by well-modedness if the inequalities are strongly covered by the modes, admissibility requires that no variable is consumed more than once. Whether this is the case depends on programming style to a certain degree, as the following example, permutation of lists, illustrates:

8.1.1 EXAMPLE: *Explicit Selectors*

p_1: perm([],[]).
p_2: perm(L,[H|T]) $\leftarrow$ append^2(V,[H|U],L), append^1(V,U,W), perm(W,T).

The superscripts of append refer to different modes. We have

mode(append^1(+,+,-)).
mode(append^2(-,-,+)).

The following definition of perm^2 specifies the same algorithm with a slightly different shape due to the use of explicit selectors and constructors:

p_1': perm^2([],[]).
p_2': perm^2(L$_1$,L$_2$) $\leftarrow$ split(L$_1$,S), car(S,V), cdadr(S,U), caadr(S,H), append(V,U,W), perm^2(W,T), cons(H,T,L$_2$).

s_1: split(L,[[],L]).
s_2: split([H|L3],[[H|L1],L2]) $\leftarrow$ split(L3,[L1,L2]).

c_1: cons(A,B,[A|B]).
c_2: car([A|B],A).
c_3: cdr([A|B],B).
c_4: cadr([A,B|_],B).
c_5: caadr([_,[B|_]|_],B).
c_6: cdadr([_,[_|B]|_],B).

Another difference is that append[2] has been replaced by the procedure split which has one output argument instead of two. This way of writing down the split procedure, exhibiting a rather unusual style from a logic programming point of view, could be the result of the compilation of a LISP program into Horn clause logic. Whereas the dataflow in the body of p_2 is rather transparent, this is not the case for p_2'. What is presented as part of a compound term in p_2 has to be retrieved by explicit use of selectors in p_2'. A consequence is that whereas the AND/OR dataflow graph corresponding to p_2 is itself an admissible solution graph, there is no admissible solution graph for the body of p_2'. The reason is that the variable S in the body of p_2', representing the terms V and [H|U] in the body of p_2, is consumed three times.

The AND/OR dataflow graphs corresponding to p_2 and p_2' are shown in figure 8.1.2.

The unfolding of the literals car(S,V), cdadr(S,U), caadr(S,H) and cons(H,T,L2) in p_2' gives the following clause p_2^*:

p_2^*: perm^2(X,[Y|Z]) ← split(X,[U,[Y|V]|W]), app(U,V,X1), perm^2(X1,Z).

The clause p_2^* now has an admissible solution graph. With p_2' replaced by p_2^* there is no problem for algorithm 7.4.5 to find out the fact that perm[2] is safe for mode(perm^2(+,-)) and to derive the valid inequality perm$^2_1$ ≥ perm$^2_2$.

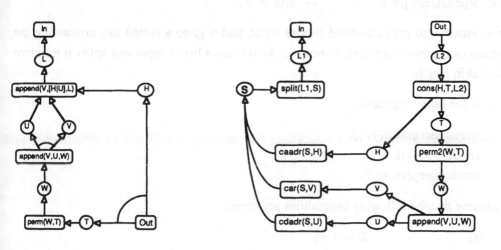

8.1.2 FIGURE: *AND/OR dataflow graphs for p_2 and p_2'*

8.2 Improving Inequalities by Unfolding

Even if it is possible to derive a linear inequality for a predicate, this inequality might be weaker than it should be. This is the case in the following example which specifies mergesort. It is taken from [ULG88].

8.2.1 EXAMPLE: *Improving Inequalities: Merge Sort*

m_1:   mergesort([],[]).

m_2:   mergesort([E],[E]).

m_3:   mergesort([E,F|U],V)   ← s([E,F|U],W,Y),
                                        mergesort(W,X), mergesort(Y,Z),
                                        merge(X,Z,V).

m_4:   merge(X,[],X).

m_5:   merge([],X,X).

m_6:   merge([A|X],[B|Y],[A|Z])   ← A=<B, merge(X,[B|Y],Z).

m_7:   merge([A|X],[B|Y],[B|Z])   ← A>B, merge([A|X],Y,Z).

m_8:   s([],[],[]).

m_9:   s([E|U],[E|V],W)   ← s(U,W,V).

Merge assumes to get two sorted lists as input, and it gives a sorted list, containing the elements of the two input lists, as output. *Split* takes a list as input and splits it into two lists of akin length.

We have the following modes:

        mode(mergesort(+,-)).
        mode(s(+,-,-)).
        mode(merge(+,+,-)).

We assume that the following inequalities are given:

        s_1 $\geq s_2 + s_3$
        $merge_1 + merge_2$ $\geq merge_3$.

The last inequality, however, is not needed.

The problem is to show that *mergesort* terminates. To this end it has to be shown that

$$|[E,F|U]\sigma| \quad > \quad |W\sigma| \qquad\qquad \text{and}$$
$$|[E,F|U]\sigma| \quad > \quad |Y\sigma|$$

for any instantiation σ satisfying s([E,F|U],W,Y). The inequality for s, however, does not imply these inequalities. It does imply the weaker inequalities

$$|[E,F|U]\sigma| \quad \geq \quad |W\sigma|$$
$$|[E,F|U]\sigma| \quad \geq \quad |Y\sigma|$$

which is not sufficient to prove termination.

Again we can try to improve the situation by unfolding. The general idea of partial evaluation is to make use of some partial input. There is such partial input in the literal s([E,F|U],W,Y), namely [E,F|U], which prevents this literal from matching s([],[],[]), the head of clause m_8. Iterated unfolding gives the following single clause m_3', which can safely replace m_3:

m_3': mergesort([X,Y|Z],U) $\leftarrow$ s(Z,V,W),
mergesort([X|V],X1),
mergesort([Y|W],Y1),
merge(X1,Y1,U).

For this clause, the given inequality for split does imply

$$|[X,Y|Z]\sigma| \quad > \quad |[X|V]\sigma|$$
$$|[X,Y|Z]\sigma| \quad > \quad |[Y|W]\sigma|$$

for appropriate instantiations σ, which is just what is needed to prove termination of mergesort.

8.3 Elimination of *'Bad'* Clauses

Suppose the following situation: there is a procedure $\pi = \{C_1,...,C_n\}$ for a predicate p. There is either no non trivial valid linear inequality for π or at least none which is strong enough for the given purpose. Now consider the procedure $\pi' = \{C_2',...,C_n'\}$

which defines a predicate p'; C_i' (for $2 \leq i \leq n$) is derived from C_i by replacing all occurrences of p by p'. Assume that the inequality, which was desired for p, can be derived for p' and in the given context one can be sure that the clause C_1 can never be applied. This is the situation where we would informally call C_1 a *bad clause*. C_1 is bad because a) it prevents deriving the inequality needed, and b) itself it is not needed at all in the given context.

8.3.1 Example: *Minimum Sort*

ms_1:   min_sort([],[]).

ms_2:   min_sort(L,[X|L1])   ← min$_1$(X,L), remove(X,L,L2),
                                              min_sort(L2,L1).

ms_3:   min$_1$(M,[X|L])   ← min$_2$(X,M,L).

ms_4:   min$_2$(X,X,[]).

ms_5:   min$_2$(X,A,[M|L])   ← min(X,M,B), min$_2$(B,A,L).

ms_6:   min(X,Y,X)   ← X =< Y .

ms_7:   min(X,Y,Y)   ← X > Y.

ms_8:   remove(N,[],[]).

ms_9:   remove(N,[N|L],L).

ms_{10}: remove(N,[M|L],[M|L1]) ← N =\= M, remove(N,L,L1).

We have the following modes:

> mode(min_sort(+,-).
> mode(min$_1$(-,+)).
> mode(min$_2$(+,-,+)).
> mode(min(+,+,-))
> mode(remove(+,+,-)).

The procedure min_sort sorts a list by iteratively searching for the minimal element of a list. Searching for a minimal element is done by min$_1$ which itself is based on m_2. The procedure *remove* removes an item from a list if this item is element of that list, otherwise the input list remains unchanged.

To prove termination of min_sort, we have to show that

(a) $|L\sigma|$ $>$ $|L2\sigma|$

for all instantiations σ which satisfy *remove(X,L,L2)*. We have only to consider the inequality for remove. This is

(b) $remove_2$ $\geq$ $remove_3$.

Inequality (b) is too weak to prove inequality (a). One would need strict inequality in (b). Strict inequality, however, cannot be derived because of clause ms_8 which is the exit clause for the case where the item which is to be *'removed'* is not element of that list. In this case the length of the list remains unchanged, whereas in all other cases it is shortened. Since in the given context of ms_2 remove(X,L,L2) is always called with X being the minimum of L, clause ms_8 will never be applied there.

Now let us render precise the argument given above. Let member(A,B) be the predicate which is true if the item A is member of the list B. We then have:

(c) $\forall$ M, L: $min_1(M,L)$ $\Rightarrow$ member(M,L)

(d) $\forall$ E, L_1, L_2: member(E,L_1) $\land$ remove(E,L_1,L_2) $\Rightarrow$ $|L_1\sigma| < |L_2\sigma|$

Walther has given an approach to mechanize this form of reasoning in [WAL88], where we took the example from. We hold, however, that this way of reasoning is very tedious to implement since it involves (1) the guess that the member predicate could be useful in this context, (2) a proof of (c) and (3) a proof of (d). Note that such proofs have their own termination problems.

The following method seems to be easier and more straightforward: Find out if there is a 'bad' clause, remove it, and derive an inequality for what remains. Identifying ms_8 as a bad clause requires (i) recognizing that without ms_8 a stronger inequality could be derived, and (ii) proving that ms_8 can never be applied in the context of ms_2.

Task (i) is quite simple. As def. 7.2.3 shows, the upper bound for the offset of a linear inequality is normally given by the nonrecursive clauses. Thus the search for 'bad' clauses can be focussed on them.

Task (ii) needs something like an inductive proof. For the given example such a proof is illustrated by figure 8.3.4. This figure shows an unfolding tree for the clause ms_2. To save space, the head of the clause and the literal min_sort(L_2,L_1), which is irrelevant in this context, is omitted. According to def. 3.5.2 and theorem 3.5.5 the branch ending in node 8 needs no further consideration since it is a failing branch. The branches having nodes numbered 3 and 6 need no further consideration, either, since none of their predicates depends on *remove*. The nodes 10 and 11 are symmetric, thus it is sufficient to discuss one of them. To prove the contrary assume that the goal of node 10 has a nonfailing branch with an application of clause ms_8. The goal of node 4 subsumes that of node 10. Application of ms_8 in the subtree rooted in node 4 leads into a failing branch, contradicting the assumption.

We next give a general specification of situations where a clause can be safely eliminated.

8.3.2 DEFINITION: *Complete Unfolding-Tree*

An unfolding-tree $T(g)$ for a goal g is a (possibly incomplete) SLD-tree.

An unfolding-tree $T(g)$ is complete for some predicate p if for each non-failing branch with leaf node e which reaches p the following holds:

- the goal e, regarded as a set of literals, is the disjoint union of e^1 and e^2 such that:
  - e^2 does not reach p
  - there is an ancestor node a of e such that $a\sigma = e^1$ for some substitution σ
  - all literals in a reaching p are p-literals, and each of them is unfolded in the subtree of $T(g)$ rooted in a.

8.3.3 THEOREM: *Complete Unfolding Trees and Redundant Clauses*

Let $T(g)$ be an unfolding tree which is complete for p and C a clause in the definition of p. If p is not applied in $T(g)$ then C does not occur in any SLD-derivation of g.

PROOF: By contradiction. Let $g = g_0,...,g_i, g_{i+1},...,g_n = \square$ be an SLD-derivation for g. Let us call it D. Assume that g_{i+1} is derived from g_i and C_i using the substitution σ_{i+1}. As mentioned in chapter 2, existence of an SLD-derivation does not depend on the computation rule. Thus we can assume, that the computation rule on which D is based and the one underlying $T(g)$ are the same. Thus there must exist a branch B of $T(g)$ which is a prefix of D. Let B be $g_0,...,g_j$. Several cases can be distinguished:

Case 1: $j > i$. Then we have that C is applied in $T(g)$ which yields a contradiction.
Case 2: $j \le i$:
Case 2a: There is no literal in g_j which reaches p. This gives a contradiction.

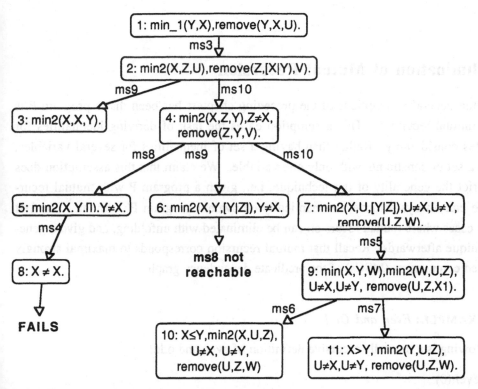

8.3.4 FIGURE *Unfolding tree for min_sort*

Case 2b: The literal p can be reached from g_j. Let $g_j{}^1$ be the subgoal of g_j which corresponds to e^1, and g_k the ancestor node corresponding to a in def. 8.3.2. According to this def. g_k is more general than $g_j{}^1$. If the head of C matches a literal of g_k, the corresponding branch of T(g) is a failure branch. This contradicts the assumption that there is a nonfailing descendant of g_j resulting from an application of C. ∎

The proof of theorem 8.3.3 uses an idea of [KUR87] where a related result has been reached for *complete pattern sets*. In this paper Kursawe has studied the question under which conditions a set of instances of a given *literal* is complete for a predicate p in the sense that it covers all possible solutions of a call to p. Theorem 8.3.3 in contrast makes a statement about the redundancy of *clauses*. It shows, for instance, that clause ms_8 is redundant in the given context although the literal remove(Z,Y,V) in node 4 of the tree in figure 8.3.4 matches the head of ms_8.

8.4 Elimination of Mutual Recursion

One of the general assumptions of the preceding chapters has been that a program P is free of mutual recursion. This assumption eases the task of deriving inequalities for predicates considerably. Rather than having a set of inequalities for several variables, there is a set of constraints with only one variable. We claim that this assumption does not restrict the generality of our technique, i.e., given a program P with mutual recursion, we can always achieve a semantically equivalent program P' without. We first identify cases where mutual recursion can be eliminated with unfolding, and give a general technique afterwards. Recall that mutual recursion corresponds to maximal strongly connected components (MSCs) of the predicate dependency graph.

8.4.1 EXAMPLE: *Even and Odd*

The following is a mutually recursive definition of even and odd:

e_1:   even(0).
e_2:   even(s(X))   ← odd(X).
e_3:   odd(s(X))   ← even(X).

Unfolding of the first literals of e_2 and e_4 gives the following equivalent procedures which have only direct recursion:

e_1':   even(0).
e_2':   even(s(s(X)))   ← even(X).

e_3':   odd(s(0)).
e_4':   odd(s(s(X)))   ← odd(X).

Equivalence of both programs is a direct consequence of theorem 3.5.5.

8.4.2 EXAMPLE: *A Parser for Arithmetical Expressions*

Consider the contextfree, non-left-recursive grammar for arithmetic expressions with the following productions:

p_1:   E → T | T + E

p_2:   T → N | N * T

p_3:   N → Z | (E)

p_4:   Z → a | b | c

Straightforward translation into Prolog yields the following program:

c_1:   e(L,T)   ←   t(L,T).

c_2:   e(L,T)   ←   t(L,['+'|C]), e(C,T).

c_3:   t(L,T)   ←   n(L,T).

c_4:   t(L,T)   ←   n(L,['*'|C]), t(C,T).

c_5:   n([L|T],T)   ←   z(L).

c_6:   n(['('|A],B)   ←   e(A,[')'|B]).

c_7:   z(a).

c_8:   z(b).

c_9:   z(c).

A query e(L,T) will give T = [] iff L is a well formed arithmetic expression according to the given grammar.

This program is mutually recursive since e $\underset{\pi}{\twoheadrightarrow}$ t $\underset{\pi}{\twoheadrightarrow}$ n $\underset{\pi}{\twoheadrightarrow}$ e, see also figure 8.4.5. An attempt to eliminate mutual recursion by unfolding would fail. It is not possible, for instance, to eliminate the call of t in c_2 since t does not only depend on n but also on itself. There is, however, an alternative to unfolding as the following program illustrates.

c_1':   parse(L,T,e)   ←   parse(L,T,t).

c_2':   parse(L,T,e)   ←   parse(L,['+'|C],t), parse(C,T,e).

c_3':   parse(L,T,t)   ←   parse(L,T,n).

c_4':   parse(L,T,t)   ←   parse(L,['*'|C],n), parse(C,T,t).

c_5':   parse([L|T],T,n)   ←   z(L).

c_6':   parse(['('|A],B,n)   ←   parse(A,[')'|B],e).

c_7':   z(a).

c_8':   z(b).

c_9':   z(c).

The transformation has been done by introducing a new predicate parse extending and replacing the former predicates e, t, and n. Differentiation between what has been replaced is done by the last argument. We claim that our idea to eliminate mutual recursion this way works in all cases. This claim is justified by a theorem of Stepanek, Stepankova and Ochozka (see [STS87]). One definition is necessary beforehand.

8.4.3 DEFINITION: *Extending a logic program*

A logic program P' extends a logic program P if the following holds:

- The language of P' contains all constants and function symbols of the language of P. Thus all terms of P are terms of P', too.
- The predicate symbols of P are mapped onto the predicate symbols of P' in the following manner:
  - Primitive predicates, i.e., predicates that are not defined in P, are the same in both programs.
  - If p is an n-ary predicate defined by P, then there is a natural number k, an n+k-predicate p' and terms $s_1,\ldots,s_k$ in the language of P' such that

    P solves the goal $p(t_1,\ldots,t_n)$ *iff*   P' solves $p(s_1,\ldots,s_k,t_1,\ldots,t_n)$ (*)
    for arbitrary terms $t_1,\ldots,t_n$ in the language of P. ∎

Note that the terms $s_1,\ldots,s_k$ depend on the predicate symbol p, but not on the terms $t_1,\ldots,t_n$ in (*).

8.4.4 THEOREM: *Normal Forms of Programs*

There is an extension in normal form of an arbitrary pure logic program P such that for every pair G, G' of corresponding goals we have

- P' solves G' in the same number of steps as P solves G.
- The corresponding arguments of G and G' receive identical values at every step of computation. ∎

Normal form in the vein of [STS87] includes the fact that there is at most one recursive predicate in P. A proof of the theorem can be found in [OSS88].

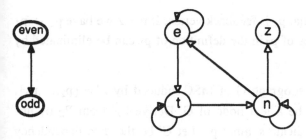

8.4.5 FIGURE: *Predicate Dependency Graphs for even/odd and parsing*

We come back to example 8.4.2. To prove the termination of parse one will first recognize that the following inequality holds:

$$parse_1 \geq parse_2.$$

To see that parse terminates in the mode($parse(+,-,+)$), problems arise from clauses c_1' - c_4' because of the identity of the first argument. These problems can be un-ravelled by assigning appropriate weights to the new constant symbols e, t and n. If we have, for instance, $|e|=3$, $|t|=2$, and $|n|=1$, we can derive termination of *parse* with a lexicographic ordering on its first and third argument.

Whereas the technique of eliminating mutual recursion suggested by theorem 8.4.4 is completely general, it has some disadvantages. The main disadvantage is that it levels out all the predicates which are in the same MSC of the predicate dependency graph. This might filter out informations which are needed for a termination proof. Unfolding, in contrast, keeps procedure definitions apart. Theorem 8.4.6 gives suffi-cient conditions for the applicability of the unfolding technique. Recall that a feedback vertex of a directed graph G is a vertex contained in every cycle of G. A linear-time algorithm for finding all feedback vertices has been given by Garey and Tarjan in [GAT78].

8.4.6 THEOREM: *Elimination of Mutual Recursion by Unfolding*

Let $\Sigma = \{p_1,...,p_n\}$ be the set of predicates which belong to the same maximal strongly connected component MSC of the predicate dependency graph of a program P, and $P_\Sigma \subseteq P$ the set of clauses of P defining predicates of Σ. If MSC has a feedback vertex $p \in \Sigma$ then mutual recursion in P_Σ can be eliminated by unfolding. ∎

PROOF: By induction on n. Assume that p_1 is feedback vertex. If $n = 2$ we have $p_2 \rightrightarrows_\pi p_1$ but not $p_2 \rightrightarrows_\pi p_2$. Thus all occurrences of p_2 in the definition of p_1 can be eliminated by unfolding.

For the inductive case, consider the subgraph G of MSC induced by $\Sigma' = \{p_2,\ldots,p_n\}$. G is a directed acyclic graph. Let p be a leaf node of G. Derive P_{Σ}' from P_Σ by unfolding all body-literals with the predicate symbol p. Let G' be the data dependency graph for P_{Σ}'. No cycle of G' contains p, thus all maximal strongly connected components of G' have less than n nodes. The induction assumption then implies that mutual recursion can safely be eliminated from P_{Σ}'. ∎

8.5 Termination of Unfolding

In 3.5 it has already been pointed out that unfolding is essentially the same as SLD-resolution. For unfolding, however, there is only partial input if at all, so it cannot be expected that the top level goal is well moded. Thus there is a severe problem of termination, where the concepts derived so far cannot be applied.

In the context of compilation and optimization, one often differentiates between literals which can be evaluated and others which cannot. Literals with a recursive predicate are normally not allowed to be evaluated (see, for instance, [VEN84]). Such an approach would be too restrictive for our purposes, as the examples 8.2.1 and 8.3.1 show.

The examples given above suggest that the following rules for unfolding might be appropriate:

(i)   Unfolding of literals with non-recursive predicates is always allowed.

(ii) Unfolding of literals with recursive predicates is allowed if it is generalizing.

Unfolding is generalizing if the p-literal which is replaced is a proper instance of the p-literals which are introduced by unfolding, for any recursive predicate p. An example for case (i) has been given in example 8.1.1. Predicates like car, cdr etc. are all non-recursive. An example for case (ii) has been given in example 8.2.1. The literal s([E,F|U],W,Y), which has been removed, is a proper instance of the literal s(Z,V,W'), which has been introduced. The justification for rule (ii) would be that the *'is-a-proper-instance-of'*-relation in the set of terms is well founded.

The conjecture that both of these rules guarantee termination is wrong, however, as the following example shows.

8.5.1 EXAMPLE: *Nonterminating Unfolding I*

t_1: $t(X)$ $\leftarrow$ $q(f(X)), q(X)$.

t_2: $q(f(f(Y)))$ $\leftarrow$ $q(Y)$.

t_3: $q(a)$.

There is an infinite SLD-tree for the goal $\leftarrow q(f(X)), q(X)$ computed according to rule (ii); a part of that tree is shown in figure 8.5.5. The reason why unfolding of t_1 does not terminate is that whereas the first p-literal is generalized, the second one is instantiated, or vice versa.

One might try to put this problem down to the cause that literals with the same predicate are building up each other. To forbid this is not sufficient as the following example shows:

8.5.2 EXAMPLE: *Nonterminating Unfolding II*

a_1: $a(X)$ $\leftarrow$ $b(f(X))$.

a_2: $b(Y)$ $\leftarrow$ $c(Y), b(Y)$.

a_3: $b(a)$.

a_4: $c(f(Z))$.

Unfolding of $b(f(X))$ according to the rules given above yields an infinite tree again. A part of it is shown in figure 8.5.5.

The two examples given above also serve to motivate the rule which we will give in the following: It is not sufficient to require that unfolding of recursive literals is generalizing. Moreover, the fact has to be established that the unfolding of a *'small'* literal and the instantiation induced by it is not taken as an excuse for the unfolding a *'big'* literal which otherwise would not be instantiated sufficiently. *Small* and *big* refer to an ordering which extends $>_\pi$ and the 'is-a-proper-instance-of'-relation. In the latter example, within the goal $\leftarrow c(Y), b(Y)$ the second literal cannot be generalized by unfolding. Unfolding of $c(Y)$ instantiates $b(Y)$ to $b(f(Z))$. This literal would be generalized by unfolding, but this has to be forbidden to prevent an infinite loop.

8.5.3 DEFINITION: *Well-founded Ordering on Goals*

In the language of a program P without mutual recursion we define the following orderings:

$>_\pi$: is a partial ordering on predicates such that

$$p >_\pi q \iff p \overset{*}{\underset{\pi}{\rightharpoonup}} q \land p \neq q.$$

$>_\delta$: is any total ordering on predicates which extends $>_\pi$.

$>_\mu$: is a partial ordering on terms such that

$t_1 >_\mu t_2 \iff$ both t_1 and t_2 have no multiple variable occurrences and there is a σ such that $t_2\sigma = t_1$; the restriction of σ to $var(t_2)$ is not only a renaming.

$\gg_\mu$: is the multiset ordering induced by $>_\mu$.

$>_\gamma$: is a partial ordering on literals such that

$$p(\tilde{r}) >_\gamma q(\tilde{s}) \iff p >_\delta q \lor (p = q \land \tilde{r} \gg_\mu \tilde{s}).$$

$\gg_\gamma$: is the multiset ordering induced by $>_\gamma$. ∎

8.5.4 PROPOSITION: *The ordering $\gg_\gamma$ is well founded.*

PROOF: Well-foundedness of $\gg_\gamma$ is implied by the well-foundedness of $>_\gamma$. The length of a sequence $t_0 >_\gamma t_1 >_\gamma \dots$ is bounded by $n*k$, where k is the number of predicates and n is the number of function symbol occurrences in t_0. ∎

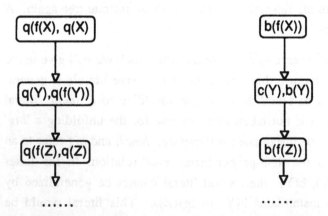

8.5.5 FIGURE *OR-tree for example 8.5.1 and 8.5.2*

We next define $\vdash_{\overline{\gamma}}$ - derivations which are SLD-derivations together with a special constraint which guarantees that the $\gg_\gamma$-ordering is satisfied. The idea is to exclude that the reduction of 'small' literals instantiates 'big' literals.

8.5.6 DEFINITION: $\vdash_{\overline{\gamma}}$ - Derivations

Let the multiset $g_{MS} = \{G_1 \times \sigma_1,\ldots,G_i \times \sigma_i,\ldots,G_n \times \sigma_n\}$ be the representation of a definite goal $g = \leftarrow G_1\sigma_1,\ldots,G_i\sigma_i,\ldots,G_n\sigma_n$ in the language of a program P where the G_i are literals and the σ_i are substitutions. Let $G_i\sigma_i = p(\bar{r})$ be the selected atom of g, $C = p(\bar{t}) \leftarrow L_1,\ldots,L_m$ a clause in P. Suppose that there exists a most general unifier θ for $p(\bar{r})$ and $p(\bar{t})$ and that

$$G_i >_\gamma L_j\theta \text{ for } j\in \{1,\ldots,m\}. \tag{+}$$

Then we write $g_{MS}\vdash_{\overline{\gamma}}g_{MS}'$, where $g_{MS}'= N_1\cup N_2\cup N_3\cup N_4\cup N_5$ and

$$N_1 = \{L_1\theta\times\varepsilon,\ldots,L_m\theta\times\varepsilon\} \tag{i}$$
$$N_2 = \{G_j\theta\times\sigma_j \mid j\neq i \wedge \sigma_j=\varepsilon \wedge \text{pred}(G_j) <_\delta p\} \tag{ii}$$
$$N_3 = \{G_j\theta\times\sigma_j \mid j\neq i \wedge \sigma_j=\varepsilon \wedge \text{pred}(G_j) = p \wedge G_j\theta \cong G_j\} \tag{iii}$$
$$N_4 = \{G_j\times\theta \mid j\neq i \wedge \sigma_j=\varepsilon \wedge \text{pred}(G_j) >_\delta p \wedge G_j\theta >_\gamma G_j\} \tag{iv}$$
$$N_5 = \{G_j\times\sigma_j\theta \mid j\neq i \wedge \sigma_j\neq\varepsilon \} \tag{v}$$

There $A \cong B$ holds iff $A\sigma$ and $B\sigma$ are identical for some variable renaming substitution σ. ∎

8.5.7 THEOREM: *The relation $\vdash_{\overline{\gamma}}$ is a well founded partial ordering.*

PROOF: Let g_{MS} and g_{MS}' be defined as in 8.5.6 and $\bar{g}$ denote the multiset $\bar{g} = \{G \mid G\times\sigma \in g\}$. We claim that

$$g_{MS}\vdash_{\overline{\gamma}}g_{MS}' \Rightarrow \bar{g}_{MS}\gg_\gamma\bar{g}_{MS}'. \tag{*}$$

Let

$$M_1 = \{G_i\times\sigma_i\} \text{ and}$$
$$M_2 = \{G_1\times\sigma_1,\ldots,G_{i-1}\times\sigma_{i-1},G_{i+1}\times\sigma_{i+1},\ldots,G_n\times\sigma_n\}$$

We have $g_{MS} = M_1 \cup M_2$ and $g_{MS}' = \bigcup_{i=1}^{5} N_i$ where the N_i are specified as in 8.5.6.

For N_1, condition (+) in 8.5.6 implies

$$\overline{M}_1 \gg_\gamma \overline{N}_1. \tag{a}$$

For each $G_j\theta \times \sigma_j \in N_2$ we have $p >_\delta \text{pred}(G_j)$, where p is the predicate of G_i. This implies $G_i >_\gamma G_j\theta$ and thus in particular we have

$$\overline{M}_1 \gg_\gamma \overline{N}_1 \cup \overline{N}_2. \tag{b}$$

For the elements $G_j\theta \times \sigma_j$ of N_3 we have $\text{pred}(G_j) = p$, and that θ is a renaming substitution for G_j, and $G_j \times \sigma_j$ is in M_2. The elements of N_4 and N_5 have the form $G_j \times \sigma_j\theta$ where $G_j \times \sigma_j$ is in M_2. This implies

$$\overline{M}_2 \cong^* \overline{N}_3 \cup \overline{N}_4 \cup \overline{N}_5, \tag{c}$$

where $\cong^*$ denotes equality on multisets modulo variable renaming. Now (b) and (c) imply (*).

8.5.8 DEFINITION: γ–Derivation Tree

For a goal g_0 a γ-derivation tree T for g_0 satisfies the following conditions:

* The root of T is $g_0 \times \varepsilon$
* If g_i is the father of g_j, then $g_i \vdash_\gamma g_j$.

Let T' be a partial SLD-tree for g_0, f a function which transforms a goal into a multiset of its literals, and h a mapping from the nodes of T to multisets of literals which is defined as follows:

$h(g) = \{L\theta \mid L \times \theta \in g\}$. Then T' corresponds to T if the following holds:

* $h(r) = f(r')$ where r is the root of T and r' is the root of T'.
* Let g_i a node of T and g_i' a node of T'. If $h(g_i) = f(g_i')$ and g_{i+1}' is a son of g_i', then there is a son g_{i+1} of g_i with $h(g_{i+1}) = f(g_{i+1}')$. ∎

8.5.9. COROLLARY: Finite Partial SLD-Trees

A partial SLD-tree for a goal g is finite if it corresponds to a γ-derivation tree for $g \times \varepsilon$.

PROOF: Corollary 8.5.9 is immediately implied by 8.5.7. ∎

8.6 Comparison with Related Work

Our technique to prove termination shares its basic approach with that proposed by Ullman and van Gelder in their recent JACM paper [ULG88]. They are concerned with the implementation of knowledge-base management systems and study the question whether the top-down, Prolog-like evaluation of recursive rules can be guaranteed to terminate. They identify the problem of local variables and apply "interargument inequalities" to this problem. Interargument inequalities have the format

$$P_i \geq P_j + x$$

where x is an integer, P is a predicate symbol, and P_i and P_j are argument designators. That is, single arguments, not sets of arguments as in our approach, are compared. This restriction means that neither the append nor the perm and the quicksort example fit in this format. Another point is that only lists are considered which are measured by their length. Rules must have the "uniqueness property" which essentially means that variables must not have more than one generator.

As the authors explicitly state, efficiency has been a major concern. From the beginning, they consider sets of predicates which are mutually recursive. To cope with mutual recursion, linear optimization techniques have to be applied. The restrictions mentioned above seem to be crucial to keep their approach efficient.

In this regard we have taken a different approach. First of all we have simplified the problem by assuming that all recursion is direct. A second step was to demonstrate that mutual recursion can be eliminated by static program transformation.

Ullman and van Gelder have suggested the following questions as appropriate for future research:

" (1) Can we extend the techniques suggested here to the case in which sizes are measured by termsize or height ...?

(2) What happens if we allow more general forms of inequalities, such as

$$P_i + P_j \leq P_k + x \quad \text{and} \quad P_i \leq P_j + P_k + x,$$

where P_i, P_j, and P_k are arguments of one predicate? 'Divide and conquer' algorithms normally require this generalization. ...

(3) Can we extend these methods to nonunique rules? ...

(4) Can we develop stronger algorithms that make use of the values of variables and arguments rather than just their sizes?

(5) We may fail to detect termination by neglecting unification issues. ... Can rules be transformed mechanically so that a subgoal q (as it appears in a rule) unifies with the left side of every rule for q?"

In this book answers were given to all of these questions. The problems (1) - (3) do not arise in our approach because it is more general. The other two have been attacked by the integration of unfolding techniques. The minimum sort example, for instance, refers to the values of variables in order to derive that the first clause for remove is a 'bad' clause. Transformation of the mergesort procedure is an example for (5).

Much research on termination proofs with well-founded orderings has been done in the context of term rewriting systems, see [DER87] for an overview. Most of the orderings used in this context are simplification orderings as defined in 3.4. The quicksort procedure in LISP notation, which has been given in 5.3.2, is an example where every simplification ordering fails to verify termination. Recall that in this example we had the two recursive calls:

(i)   `(qsort(car(split (car L) (cdr L))))`   and

(ii)   `(qsort(cdr(split (car L) (cdr L))))`.

Simplification orderings have the replacement and the subterm property:

(a) $t > t'$ implies $f(...t...) > f(...t'...)$

(b) $f(...t...) > t$.

Considering (i), (b) implies `(cdr (split (car L) (cdr L))) > L`, hence (a) implies `(qsort (car (split (car L) (cdr L)))) > (qsort L)`. Thus termination of the qsort procedure in 5.3.2 cannot be verified with a simplification ordering.

On the other hand, taking the recursive path ordering as an example for a simplification ordering, the rule of distributivity

s_i: $s(X * (Y + Z), T) \leftarrow s(X * Y + X * Z, T)$.

illustrates the relative strength of such an ordering compared with our approach, at least as far as linear norms are concerned. For an arbitrary linear norm, as defined in 3.4, we have

$$| X * Y + X * Z | \geq | X * (Y + Z) |.$$

Taking '*' > '+' as precedence we have

$$X * (Y + Z) >_{rpo} X * Y + X * Z.$$

If, however, the first argument is input of the clause s_i given above, there are no local variables. Hence predicate inequalities are not needed. There is no problem to combine the RPO technique with ours.

Chapter 9

CONCLUSIONS

Termination proofs for recursive procedures amount to demonstrating that the recursive instance of a problem is smaller than the problem originally given. In the context of logic programming such proofs are often straightforward if recursive clauses have no new variables on the input positions of their recursive literals. Any simplification ordering may be used to verify the fact that the terms occurring in recursive calls become smaller according to a well-founded ordering. Occurrences of local variables, however, pose difficulties. This book takes a semantic approach to overcome these difficulties. We give an algorithm which derives linear inequalities for predicates and applies them in termination proofs. Contrary to what one might expect in the context of deductive systems this algorithm needs no guidance from the user. It assumes that the program is well-moded, normalized and has no mutual recursion. Normalization and well-modedness of programs are achieved by well-known techniques. That mutual recursion can be eliminated by static program transformation has been demonstrated above. On the further assumption that there are bounds on the structure of the clauses, the running time of our algorithm is linear in the length of the program. Practical experience has demonstrated that the performance of this technique is sufficient to incorporate it in an advanced Prolog programming environment, as being developed in the PROTOS project.

Linear predicate inequalities refer to the minimal Herbrand model of a program. They do not need information on operational aspects. Termination proofs, in contrast, refer to the operational semantics of a program. In this book we have mainly considered Prolog's search strategy based on SLD-resolution. This is just one, albeit important, application of linear predicate inequalities. They can also be used to give a sufficient criterion for programs which have the bounded term size property, thus answering an open research problem which has been posed in the context of deductive databases.

Another interesting application is goal-directed forwardchaining (GDFC), a technique proposed by Yanamoto and Tanaka in [YAT86]. It was extended and improved by Burgard in [BUR89]. GDFC, which is implemented on top of (pure) Prolog, essentially means that the generation of logical consequences of a program is focussed on the derivation of a given goal. It has been an open problem how termination can be achieved for GDFC if recursion and function symbols are at hand. In his diploma thesis Heidelbach describes a safe and complete implementation of GDFC with a termination criterion which is based on linear predicate inequalities (see [HEI90]).

The approach taken in this book has several advantages relative to what has been previously described. In contrast to many techniques proposed in the context of term rewriting systems, it is basically a semantic approach. Thus the termination proofs derived are fairly comprehensible. Derivation of linear inequalities involves searching (for a valid inequalitiy) and verification (of the validity of that inequality). Both problems are solved by our algorithm in reasonable time. In contrast such a technique as RPO, for instance, needs a precedence among function symbols as input.

Compared with the approach taken by Ullman and van Gelder our method is more general in the format of inequalities and in the way how sizes of terms are measured. We consider inequalities which compare tuples of terms (not only single terms), and we allow any linear term norm (not only length of lists).

The advantages are illustrated by the quicksort example quoted throughout this book. To achieve a termination proof for quicksort automatically is notoriously difficult. As this algorithm is written down in example 5.3.2 simplification orderings are unable to verify termination. The technique of Ullman and van Gelder does not suffice either because of the restricted format of their inequalities.

Further work remains to be done. We have described our technique in terms of pure Prolog. Some non-pure features have already been considered. The difficulties caused by the nonlogical features of Prolog still deserve serious analysis.

An important question is how the restriction on well-moded programs can be weakened. Termination of append, for instance, does not require that it is invoked with ground lists. Lists with possibly non-ground elements suffice as well. Generalization could possibly be achieved by incorporating polymorphic type informations.

REFERENCES

[ABB86]   Aquilano, C., Barbuti, R., Bocchetti, P., Martelli, M., Negation as Failure. Completeness of the Query Evaluation Process for Horn Clause Programs with Recursive Definitions, *Journal of Automated Reasoning*, 2, 1986, 155-170.

[ABH87]   Abramsky, S., Hankin, C. (eds.), *Abstract Interpretation of Declarative Languages*, Ellis Horwood, 1987.

[ABK89]   Apt, K. R., Bol, R. N., Klop, J. W., On the Safe Termination of Prolog Programs, in: Levi, G., Martelli, M., (eds.), Proceedings of the Sixth International Conference on Logic Programming, Pisa 1989.

[ABW87]   Apt, K. R., Blair, A., Walker, A., Towards a Theory of Declarative Knowledge, in: Minker, J. (ed.), *Foundations of Deductive Databases and Logic Programming*, Morgan Kaufman, Los Altos, 1987, 89-148.

[ACH90]   Appelrath, H.-J., Cremers, A. B., Herzog, O., The EUREKA Project PROTOS, April 9, 1990, Zurich, Switzerland.

[ACS88]   Appelrath, H.-J., Cremers, A. B., Schiltknecht, H. (eds.), *PROTOS: Prolog Tools for Building Expert Systems,* First Workshop, Morcote 1988.

[AHU74]   Aho, A. V., Hopcroft, J. E., Ullman, J. D., *The Design and Analysis of Computer Algorithms*, Addison-Wesley, Reading, Mass., 1974.

[APE82]   Apt, K. R., Emden, M. H., Contributions to the Theory of Logic Programming, *Journal of the ACM*, 29, 3 (July 1982), 841-862.

[AUB79]   Aubin, R., Mechanizing Structural Induction, Part I: Formal system, *Theoretical Computer Science*, 9, 1979, 329-345.

[BAC88]   Bachmair, L., *Proof Methods for Equational Theories*, Dept. of Computer Science, SUNY at Stony Brook, New York, 1988.

[BAM87]   Barbuti, R., Martelli, M., *A Generally Functional Programming Style for Logic Databases*, Dipartimento di Informatica Universita di Pisa, Technical Report, 1987.

[BAR86]   Bancilhon, F., Ramakrishnan, R., An Amateur's Introduction to Recursive Query Processing Strategies, *Proceedings of the ACM SIGMOD International Conference on Management of Data* (Washington, D.C., May 28-30). ACM, New York, 1986, 16-52.

[BEL86]   Bellia, L., Levi, G., The Relation between Logic and Functional Languages: A Survey. *Journal of Logic Programming*, 3, 1986, 217-236.

[BLA68]   Black, F., A Deductive Question-Answering System, in: Minsky ,M. (ed.), *Semantic Information Processing*, MIT Press, Cambridge, MA, 1968, 354-402.

[BOE85]   Börger, E., *Berechenbarkeit, Komplexität, Logik*, Vieweg & Sohn, Braunschweig, 1985.

[BOE87]   Börger, E., Unsolvable Decision Problems for Prolog Programs, in: Börger, E. (ed.), *Computation Theory and Logic*, Springer LNCS 270, 1987, 37-48.

[BRW84]   Brough, D.,Walker, A., Some Practical Properties of Prolog Interpreters, *Proc. of the Japan FGCS84 Conference*, 1984, 149-156.

[BUR89]   Burgard, W., Generating a Data Structure for Goal-Directed Forward
            Chaining in Logic Programming, Forschungsbericht 331 der Abteilung
            Informatik der Universität Dortmund, 1990.

[CHL73]   Chang, C. L., Lee, R. C. T., *Symbolic Logic and Mechanical Theorem
            Proving*, Academic Press, New York, 1973.

[CLA79]   Clark, K. L., *Predicate Logic as a Computational Formalism*, Technical
            Report 79/59, Dept. of Computing, Imperial College, London, 1979.

[CLM81]   Clocksin, W. F., Mellish, C. S., *Programming in Prolog*, Springer, 1981.

[CLP86]   Cremers, A. B., Lüttringhaus, S., Plümer, L., Prolog Source Level
            Transformations for Deductive Databases, *ESPRIT Workshop on
            Integration of Logic Programming and Data Bases*, Venice, 1986, 14 pp.

[COV85]   Covington, M. A., Eliminating unwanted Loops in Prolog, *SIGPLAN
            Notices*, 20, January 1985, 20-26.

[CRE86]   Cremers, A. B., *Lecture on Artificial Intelligence*, Dortmund, 1986 (In
            German).

[CRH80]   Cremers, A. B., Hibbard, T. N., *Specification of Data Spaces by Means of
            Context-Free Grammar-Controlled Primitive Recursion*, Abteilung
            Informatik der Universität Dortmund, Forschungsbericht 107, 1980.

[DAR81]   Darlington, J., An Experimental Program Transformation and Synthesis
            System, *Artificial Intelligence*, 16, 1981, 1-46.

[DEG86]   DeGroot, D. (ed.), *Logic programming: Functions, Relations and
            Equations*, Prentice Hall, Englewood Cliffs, 1986.

[DEM79]   Dershowitz, N., Manna, Z., Proving Termination with Multiset
            Orderings, *Comm. ACM*, 22, 1979, 465-476.

[DEM85]   Dembinski,. P., Maluszynski, J., And-Parallelism with Intelligent
            Backtracking for Annotated Logic Programs, *Symposion on Logic
            Programming 1985*, Boston, 1985, 29-38.

[DER82]   Dershowitz, N., Orderings for Term-Rewriting Systems, *Theoretical
            Computer Science*, 17, 1982, 279-301.

[DER87]   Dershowitz, N., Termination of Rewriting, *Journal of Symbolic
            Computation*, 3, 1987, 69-116.

[DEW88]   Debray, S. K., Warren, D. S., Automatic Mode Inference for Logic
            Programs, *The Journal of Logic Programming*, 5, 3, 1988, 207-229.

[EMK76]   van Emden, M. H., Kowalski, R., The Semantics of Predicate Logic as a
            Programming Language, *Journal of the ACM*, 23 , 4, 1976, 733-742.

[END72]   Enderton, H. B., *A Mathematical Introduction to Logic*, Academic Press,
            New York, 1972.

[FIC88]   Ficarelli, A., *Il Problema della Terminazione in Programmazione
            Logica*, Master's Thesis, Dept. of Comp. Science, University of Pisa,
            1988 (personal communication).

[FLO66]   Floyd, R. W., Assigning Meanings to Programs, in: Schwartz, J. T. (ed.),
            Mathematical Aspects of Computer Science, Proc. Symposia in Applied
            Mathematics, Vol. XIX, 1966, Providence, Rhode Island, 1967, 19-32.

[GAT78]   Garey, M. R., Tarjan, R. E., A Linear-Time Algorithm for finding all
            Feedback Vertices, *Information Processing Letters*, 7, 1978, 274-276.

[GEL87]   van Gelder, A., Negation as Failure using Tight Derivations for General
            Logic Programs, in: Minker, J. (ed.), *Foundations of Deductive Databases
            and Logic Programming*, Morgan Kaufmann, Los Altos, 1987, 149-176.

[HEI90]   Heidelbach, M., Verfahren zur Behandlung spezieller Probleme bei der
            vorwärtsgerichteten Auswertung von logischen Programmen,
            Diplomarbeit, Universität Dortmund, 1990.

[HOG84]   Hogger, C. J., *Introduction to Logic Programming*, London, 1984.

[HOK87]   Horiuchi, K., Kanamori, T., Polymorphic Type Inference in Prolog by
            Abstract Interpretation, *Logic Programming 1987*, Springer LNCS 315,
            195-214.

[HUO80]   Huet, G., Oppen, D. C., Equations and Rewrite Rules: A Survey, in:
            Book, R. V. (ed.), *Formal Language Theory: Perspectives and Open
            Problems*, Academic Press, 1980, 349-405.

[KLE52]   Kleene, S. C., *Introduction to Metamathematics*, Van Nostrand, 1952.

[KNB70]   Knuth, D. E., Bendix, P. B., Simple Word Problems in Universal
            Algebras, in: Leech, J. (ed.), *Computational Problems in Abstract
            Algebra*, Pergamon Press, 1970, 263-297.

[KNU73]   Knuth, D. E., *The Art of Computer Programming I: Fundamental
            Algorithms*, Addison Wesley, 1973.

[KOR79]   Kowalski, R. A., Algorithm = Logic + Control, *Comm. of the ACM*, 22,
            7, 1979, 424-436.

[KOW79]   Kowalski, R. A., *Logic for Problem Solving*, North Holland, New York,
            1979.

[KUR87]   Kursawe, P., Pure Partial Evaluation and Instantiation, *Workshop on
            Partial Evaluation and Mixed Computation*, Denmark, 1987.

[LLO87]   Lloyd, J., *Foundations of Logic Programming*, Springer, Berlin, 1987.

[LLS87]   Lloyd, J. W., Shepherdson, J. C., *Partial Evaluation in Logic
            Programming*, Technical Report CS-87-09, University of Bristol, 1987.

[LOV78]   Loveland, D. W., *Automated Theorem Proving: A Logical Basis*, North
            Holland, Amsterdam, 1978.

[MAN74]   Manna, Z., *Mathematical Theory of Computation*, Mc-Graw-Hill, New
           York, 1974.

[MEL87]   Mellish, C., Abstract Interpretation of Prolog programs, in: Abramsy, S.,
           Hankin, C. (eds.), *Abstract Interpretation of Declarative languages*,
           Chichester, 1987, 181-198.

[MIN67]   Minsky, M., *Computation: Finite and Infinite Machines*, Prentice Hall,
           1967.

[MIN87]   Minker, J. (ed.), *Foundations of Deductive Databases and Logic
           Programming*, Morgan Kaufmann, Los Altos, 1987.

[MKS81]   McKay, D. P., Shapiro, S., Using active connection graphs for reasoning
           with recursive rules, in: *Proceedings Seventh International Joint
           Conference on Artificial Intelligence*, Vancouver, BC, 1981, 368-374.

[MMN75]   Milner, R., Morris, L., Newey, M., A logic for computable functions
           with reflexive and polymorphic types, in: Huet, G., Kahn, G. (eds.),
           Actes coll. Construction, Amelioration et Verification de Programmes,
           France, 1975, 371-394.

[MYK84]   Mycroft, A., O'Keefe, R. A., A Polymorphic Type System for Prolog,
           Artificial Intelligence, 23, 1984, 295-388.

[NAI86]   Naish, L., *Negation and Control in Prolog*, Springer LNCS 238, Berlin,
           1986.

[NIL82]   Nilsson, N. J., *Problem solving methods in Artificial Intelligence*, New
           York, 1982.

[OSS88]   Ochozka, V., Stepankova, O., Stepanek, P., Hric, J., Normal Forms and
           Complexity of Computations of Logic Programs, *Computer Science
           Logic*, Duisburg, 1988, Springer LNCS 385, 357-371.

[PLA84]   Plaisted, D. A., The Occur-Check Problem in Prolog, *IEEE Int. Symp.
           on Logic Programming*, Atlantic City, 1984, 272-280.

[PLU86]   Plümer, L., Und-Parallelismus und effizientes Backtracking von Prolog-
            Programmen, *16. GI-Jahrestagung*, Springer, Berlin, 1986, 137-151.

[PLU89]   Plümer, L., Termination Proofs for Logic Programs, Dissertation Thesis,
            Universität Dortmund, 1989.

[PLU90]   Plümer, L., Termination Proofs for Logic Programs based on Predicate
            Inequalities, *Seventh International Conference on Logic Programming*,
            Jerusalem, 1990.

[POG85]   Poole, D., Goebel, R., On eliminating loops in Prolog, *SIGPLAN Notices*
            20, 8, August 1985, 38-40.

[RED86]   Reddy, U. S., On the relationship between Logic and Functional
            Languages, in: DeGroot, D. (ed.), *Logic Programming: Functions,
            Relations and Equations*, Prentice Hall, Englewood Cliffs, 1986, 3-31.

[RIC87]   Ricci, F., *Zur Vermeidung divergenter Inferenz bei der Auswertung
            strukturell rekursiver Horn-Klausel-Programme*, Diplomarbeit,
            Universität Dortmund, 1987.

[ROB65]   Robinson, J. A., A Machine-Oriented Logic Based on the Resolution
            Principle, *Journal of the ACM*, 12, 1, 1965, 23-41.

[SCH74]   Schnoor, C. P., *Rekursive Funktionen und ihre Komplexität*, Stuttgart,
            1974.

[SEI88]   Seki, H., Itoh, H., A Query Evaluation Method for Stratified Programs
            under the Extended CWA, in: Kowalski, R., Bowen, K. (eds.), *Logic
            Programming*, Proceedings of the Fifth International Conference and
            Symposium, Seattle, 1988, 195-211.

[SGG87]   Smith, D. E., Genesereth, M. R., Ginsberg, M. L., Controlling Recursive
            Inference, *Artificial Intelligence*, 30, 3, 343-389.

[STS87]   Stepankova, O., Stepanek, P., Developing Logic Programs: Computing
            through Normalization, in: *Computer Science Logic 1987*, Springer
            LNCS 329, 1988, 304-321.

[TAF86]   Takeuchi, A., Furukuwa, K., Partial evaluation of prolog programs and
            its application to meta programming, in: Kugler, H.-J. (ed.), *Information
            Processing*, 86, North Holland, Dublin, 1986, 415-420.

[TAR75]   Tärnlund, S.-Å., *Logic information processing*, Report TRITA-IBADB
            1034, Dept. of Information Processing and Computer Science, The Royal
            Institute of Technology and the University of Stockholm, Sweden, 1975.

[TAS84]   Tamaki, H., Sato, T., Unfold/Fold Transformation of Logic Programs,
            Proc. Sec. Conf. on Logic Programming, Uppsala, 1984, 127-138.

[TAS86]   Tamaki, H., Sato, T., OLD resolution with tabulation, *Third International
            Conference on Logic Programming*, London, 1986, 84-98.

[ULG88]   Ullman, J. D., van Gelder, A., Efficient Tests for Top-Down
            Termination of Logical Rules, *Journal of the ACM*, 35, 2, 1988, 345-373.

[VAP86]   Vasak, T., Potter, J., Characterization of Terminating Logic Programs,
            1986 IEEE Symp. on Logic Programming, Vancouver, 140-147.

[VEN84]   Venken, Raf, A prolog meta-interpreter for partial evaluation and its
            application to source to source transformation and query optimization,
            ECAI 84: Advances in Artificial Intelligence, Pisa, 1984, 347-356.

[WAL88]   Walther, C., *Automated Termination Proofs*, Universität Karlsruhe,
            Fakultät für Informatik, Interner Bericht 17/88, 1988.

[YAT86]   Yamamoto, A., Tanaka, H., Translating Production Rules into a Forward
            Reasoning Prolog Program, New Generation Computing, 4, 1986, 37-
            105.

NOTATION

INDEX

Lecture Notes in Computer Science